Shivalik Bakshi was born in Amritsar. He is a microelectromechanical systems (MEMS) engineer. When not building microscopic-sized machines in a cleanroom, he likes to investigate the case of the men who went missing during the 1971 war. He can be contacted by email at NowhereMen1971@gmail.com.

Celebrating 35 Years of
Penguin Random House India

PENGUIN VEER

NO WHERE MAN

NOWHERE MAN

The Story of CAPTAIN KAMAL BAKSHI, Missing since the 1971 INDO–PAK WAR

SHIVALIK BAKSHI

PENGUIN
VEER

An imprint of Penguin Random House

PENGUIN VEER

USA | Canada | UK | Ireland | Australia
New Zealand | India | South Africa | China | Singapore

Penguin Veer is part of the Penguin Random House group of companies
whose addresses can be found at global.penguinrandomhouse.com

Published by Penguin Random House India Pvt. Ltd
4th Floor, Capital Tower 1, MG Road,
Gurugram 122 002, Haryana, India

First published in Penguin Veer by Penguin Random House India 2023

ISBN 9780143460411

Typeset in Adobe Caslon Pro by MAP Systems, Bengaluru, India
Printed at Thomson Press India Ltd, New Delhi

www.penguin.co.in

This book is dedicated to M. Abdul Hamid, the morally upright Pakistani gentleman who, at great personal risk, passed along a note from an Indian POW to his father, informing the latter that he was still alive even though his name was not on the list of POWs handed to the Red Cross.

Whoever you are, Mr Hamid—thank you!

Contents

Prologue

Chhamb
3 December 1971

War between India and Pakistan seems likely—the two have been provoking one another for months and now there are reports of foreign embassy staff being ordered to leave the two countries.

If fighting does indeed break out, Captain Kamal Bakshi knows he will be in it, for his battalion is tasked with defending a key section of the border. What he does not know is that his post lies in the dead centre of the largest offensive already set into play by the Pakistanis. Along the 24-kilometre-long border that defines the Chhamb sector, Pakistan is about to unleash fifteen infantry battalions, 130 artillery guns and 129 tanks.[1]

Nor does he know that when the war ends, the Battle of Chhamb will be proclaimed among the deadliest of the war of 1971, in which scores of men will have perished.

In recognition of his valour in battle, the military will announce a medal for him. But he will not accept his award in person for he will have gone missing. Although no one from his battalion will see him get killed, none will be able to locate his body either. Then, eight years after the war's ending, a government minister will announce the names of soldiers that the Indian intelligence agencies believe are still being detained in Pakistan and one of the names will be his.

This book is his story, recreated from letters, diaries and recollections of those whose paths crossed his.

1

Early Years
1945–1953

1945

It is an ordinary spring day for most residents of Rawalpindi, but for the Datta household, it is anything but. Much excitement brews there, for Nanak Chand Datta has invited Bakshi Hari Chand Chhibber and his family over for tea. Although the reason for the invitation was not expressly stated, it is understood by all involved that the meeting is to explore the possibility of marriage between Nanak Chand's daughter Shanta and Hari Chand's son Om Prakash.

When the guests arrive, Shanta is absent from the living room as per the norm of the time. Also, per these norms, it is only Kartar Devi, Om Prakash's mother, who is invited deeper into the house to meet Shanta. And while Om Prakash's mother conducts the most fateful meeting of his life on his behalf, Shanta's father does the same for her.

'I hear you were deployed overseas?' Nanak Chand asks Om Prakash.

'Ji—I have recently returned from Italy.'

'How was it over there? As bad as we read in the newspapers?'

'Ji. My unit lost many fine men. I was one of the lucky few to get away with just a couple of bullet wounds . . .'

'His wounds have healed completely,' Hari Chand interjects, not wanting to leave any doubt about his son's fitness.

More questions follow from Nanak Chand: What had Om Prakash been up to before joining the Army? Which subjects had he studied in college? What were his personal interests? And so on ...

Later that day, after returning home, Om Prakash asks his mother to recount everything that had transpired between her and Shanta. He wanted to know everything Shanta had said, how she had said it, her demeanour and on and on. To Om Prakash's final question—'Is she nice?'—his mother answers in the affirmative. '*Badi changi kudi hai* (she is a very nice girl),' she says.

Over in Nanak Chand's house, Shanta, being Shanta, has an even longer list of questions for her widowed father and every other person who was present during the meeting. To her relief, there is near-unanimous approval of Om Prakash. The lone objector is her adopted brother Darshan, who suspects that Hari Chand was not being forthright about his son's physical condition, for Om Prakash had worn tinted glasses during the entire visit, even while indoors.

'I have never seen anything like it. Surely he has some kind of a problem with his eyes,' says Darshan.

To allay Darshan's concerns, Nanak Chand makes a polite inquiry through an intermediary about the condition of the prospective groom's eyes.

'Fully operational,' comes the reply. The dark glasses are simply a modern fashion accessory that

Om Prakash had picked up during his six-month-long convalescence in the field hospital in Bagnacavallo, Italy.

So it comes to pass that Shanta and Om Prakash are betrothed. Soon after, the two families consult a priest for auspicious dates in the months ahead and settle on a day in August for the wedding.

1946

In Holy Family Hospital, Rawalpindi, a boy has been born to Shanta and Om Prakash. Besides being their firstborn, he is also the first grandchild in the family. And so a big celebration is planned and everyone is invited—neighbours, friends from the past and the present, relatives from near and far.

Although it is too early to tell whom the boy resembles most, the general consensus is that he has taken after his mother—the shape of his mouth and his piercing eyes are a dead giveaway. His father accepts that outcome good-naturedly. It is better the boy looks like his mother than like me, he says. But when it comes to naming the boy, his father is determined to have his way, for he has thought long and hard about it. He wants to name his son after Sepoy Kamal Ram,[1] a brave young soldier from his regiment who was awarded the Victoria Cross for his courageous actions in the battle for Monte Cassino in Italy. When his father recounts all the daring feats of the fearless soldier to his mother—how he had volunteered without hesitation to single-handedly silence the machine gun post that was holding back his company's advance, and then had gone on to attack a second post until the men there surrendered—she readily agrees to naming their son Kamal.

1947

July

It is his first birthday today, but no big celebration is planned, just a small ceremony in the prayer room of the house with only the family in attendance. While cradling him in her arms, his mother sings an *aarti* to invoke the gods and to seek their blessings for him. Then she distributes home-made sweets to the family and neighbours whose houses abut theirs. It is all over quickly.

The reason for keeping the celebration subdued is to not attract attention to the house, for it has become unsafe to step outside where marauding mobs troll the neighbourhoods looking for their quarry—everyone not of their faith. If the mob comes across a household of a faith other than theirs, they set the house alight. And if the occupants choose to run out of their burning house, a vengeful swordsman stands at the ready to turn them back.

In their case, a Hindu family living in a region where people of their faith are in the minority, their situation would have been dire were it not for Amjad—a brave Muslim man who is their neighbour and friend. Each night, Amjad parks himself on a cot outside their house and keeps vigil until the early hours of the morning. When a marauding mob approaches, he stands tall and calmly waves them away.

August

Punjab, the land of his birth and of his forefathers' birth, is to be cleaved into two along religious lines— the Muslim-majority western half will go to a new country called Pakistan, while the Hindu-Sikh-dominated eastern half will remain in India. Exactly where the boundary will fall, no one knows. Many residents of Rawalpindi have decided to wait for the government-appointed Boundary Commission to demarcate the border before making a move, but his father is not among them. With permission from the commanding officer of his unit in Jullundur, where he is posted, he has requisitioned a medium-sized truck to move his family from Rawalpindi to safety in East Punjab.

'Pack only the essentials,' his father tells his mother when he drives up in the truck. 'We will return for the rest when matters calm down.'

After gathering some clothes, a few cooking utensils and enough food for the long drive, they are on their way.

Their plan is to first head to Lahore to spend the night in the relative safety of a big city and then continue on to Jullundur the following day. But their progress is slow, for it is the monsoon season and the roads are flooded in many places.

His father sits up front in the driver's cabin with a revolver at the ready to engage any troublemaker, while the rest of them—he, his mother, two young aunts and their adopted brother Darshan—sit in the back. Out of caution, his father has pulled down the canvas cover of the back of the truck so as not to expose the sensitive cargo he is ferrying.

When evening approaches, the adults around him take to talking in whispers, fearful about being out on the road after dark when marauders could appear from anywhere, any time. As for their fear that the little child with them might give them away with his whining or wailing, they need not have worried. Perhaps he is concerned by the anxious faces of the adults around him, or maybe he is soothed by the continuous drone of the truck's engine; whichever it is, he is quiet and rides in silence, keeping his demands to a minimum.

1952

It has been five years since Partition and he has been on the move ever since, relocating every couple of years to wherever his father is posted. First to Jullundur, then to Delhi and now to Kashmir.

His new home sits on the banks of the river Jhelum, which he crosses twice a day by boat to get to and from his school. In the evenings he likes to play with his younger siblings. His family has grown in the intervening years. Now he has not one but two younger sisters whom he dotes on.

During the winter months, when school is out and snow blankets the Kashmir valley, his mother takes him and his sisters down to the milder climes of the plains to visit relatives. Like many refugees from Pakistan, most of his relatives have chosen to settle down in towns across the state of Punjab, while a few have moved to Delhi and to cities beyond.[i]

His maternal grandfather, a civil engineer by profession, now lives in a town called Karnal. Before the Partition, he was responsible for constructing large canals and bridges across much of Punjab and Kashmir, but now he has been forced to settle for less rewarding work like laying roads in the townships springing up across northern India to accommodate the throngs of refugees.

His paternal grandfather, on the other hand, is one of the few to have benefitted from the Partition. He had been a bank clerk up until the day of Independence, when his English manager suddenly announced that he was returning to England and was

---

[i] A relative from Rawalpindi named Anand Bakshi would end up in Mumbai, where he would make a name for himself as a poet and songwriter.

promoting his grandfather to the top post. '*Raaton-raat hum* manager *ban gaye* (I became a manager overnight),' his grandfather often tells him.

1953

It is mid-May, the hottest time of the year in Ferozepur, where they now live, and his mother has forbidden him and his sisters from playing outdoors in the searing afternoons. Only when the temperature dips in the evening does she permit them to go to the nearby playground. It is there that he demonstrates his athletic prowess to his sisters by clambering up the slides, pulling himself up the monkey bars and spinning them fast on the merry-go-round while they squeal with delight.

One day, when it is time to head home, he notices children standing around the square pit used by the park attendant to burn dry leaves in, and announces that he is going to jump across it. But his running leap is not enough to clear the pit. Although his left leg makes it across, his right leg sinks into the smouldering mass of dead leaves. There are shouts and screams. The attendant comes running and pulls him out, but not before his leg has sustained third-degree burns.

○ ○ ○

He has been in the hospital for a whole month and now the doctor has finally cleared him for discharge.

It is on the drive home that he learns of his father's upcoming military deployment overseas.

'Are you going to fight the Nazis again?' he asks his father.

'No. This time I am going to keep the peace between the Americans and the Chinese,' replies his father, who is headed to Korea to oversee the exchange of prisoners of war there. The reason he has been selected for the mission[2] is because of his expertise in speaking fluent Mandarin Chinese.

'When will you be back?'

'Sometime next year. Hopefully in time to take you to the new school we have found for you.'

'Am I changing schools again?' he asks. The news that he is changing schools again does not come as a complete surprise to him; although he is only six years old, he has switched schools twice already.

'Yes, we found a new one for you. It is called Sherwood College. It's a very nice school, and you won't have to keep changing schools any more. It is a little far from home so you will live there.'

He does not understand. Falls silent.

Major O.P. Bakshi (Kamal's father) standing at the newly
established DMZ line separating North and South Korea. He was
a member of the Custodian Force responsible for overseeing the
repatriation of prisoners of the recently ended war.

2

Boyhood
1954–1962

1954

He is walking down a long hallway, looking for dormitory number two; trailing him are his mother and his maternal grandfather who have come to see him off at his new school—Sherwood College, Nainital.

After unpacking his belongings and storing them in his assigned closet, his mother turns to him to say goodbye.

'Promise me that you will study hard.'

He promises.

'Promise me you will write to me regularly.'

He promises.

Kamal (aged seven) heading off to boarding school, with Grandpa filling in for his father, who was in Korea at that time.

ooo

He tries his hardest to be self-reliant: brushes his teeth without having to be reminded by the matron, trims his nails before being asked, ensures his shoes are always polished to a shine. But there is one thing he finds difficult to master—tying his necktie. His mind gets twisted in a knot when following the housemaster's directions, so he turns to an attendant for help.

As for his studies, he chooses to sit in the front row in class and pays complete attention to all the teachers. His favourite subject is nature studies (plants and animals and all things natural), although he does well in all subjects. In the recent English dictation test, he scored full marks, he proudly reports in a letter home.

○○○

One thing he does not like about his new school life is shower time. On the walk down the long hallway to the bathroom, the burn scar on his leg is clearly visible to everyone around him and some boys comment on its appearance. 'It's scaly, almost reptilian,' they say. He pretends their words do not bother him, but they do.

But one boy in his dormitory is different from the rest: 'Your scar seems to be getting worse. What are you going to do?' asks the boy with genuine concern.

He appreciates the boy's sincerity, his kindness and his gentle manner. In a letter home to his mother, he reports that he now has a friend.

Shahid

(Dr Shahid Najeeb is a psychiatrist and training psychoanalyst based in Australia. He was Kamal's classmate.)

[Author] *Thank you for promptly replying to my email, Dr Najeeb. I appreciate your agreeing to share your recollections of Kamal. For starters, I want to take you back to the spring of 1954. In a letter Kamal wrote to his mother back then, he mentioned having made his very first friend, a boy by the name of 'Shied'. As you know, there was nobody by that name in your class, but your name comes closest to it. Was he referring to you?*

[S] He must have misspelled my name. Both of us joined school in the same year and he was one of my first friends.

Could you share some recollections of that friendship?

What would you like to know?

Everything.

All right. From the very beginning then.

When we joined Sherwood in 1954 in Horseman Wing (Junior School), we were in the same dormitory, our beds next to each other.

We probably played and talked to each other during the day, but the evenings in bed were probably the times when we exchanged confidences. I remember that he talked a lot about horrific experiences during the Partition of India. Although I cannot remember him saying anything specifically about his family, I got the impression that they were directly involved. I felt a bit awkward and guilty because he talked about the atrocities that Muslims had committed against Hindus, and I was a Muslim. However, that did not in any way change the warm way we personally related to each other. He seemed traumatized by these events—maybe from listening to accounts of them from family members? People now talk about trans-generational trauma.

I have another vivid memory of the two of us in that first year. In the dormitory we were not allowed to talk after lights out, though as I have said, that's when we probably spoke the most! One night, our very gentle matron Miss Joyce told us to be careful not to talk after 'lights out' because the principal of the junior school had just got a new cane, which she had tried on her hand, and it really hurt. Until then, we had got the brush on our calves for punishment. But I guess boys will be boys and Kamal and

I talked after lights out that very night. We were caught, along with a couple of other boys. So we were hauled out of our beds and got caned right there in the dormitory, which was unusual, for canings were generally done in the principal's office. Perhaps this was to set an example. The cane really cut into our tender tiny bottoms and poor Kamal made the terrible mistake of running down the dormitory rubbing his bum and chuffing like a steam locomotive! Children can be very cruel and for a long time he was tormented by other boys, imitating him.

I remember two other incidents from a couple of years after our first year. We used to play 'Conkers', which was a game in which peeled chestnuts were strung from a string and you had to hit the other person's chestnut. Whoever got his chestnut broken first, lost. Often, these chestnuts would be 'seasoned' by drying and then subjected to personal, patented treatments! We got these chestnuts from local trees, but to get to the chestnut, the soft outer skin had to be peeled off. Kamal used to peel this skin with his teeth, and he developed a terrible rash around his mouth, which was very painful. Maybe sometime later or maybe before, he had a terrible rash on his calves, which he showed me, and also showed me how he was treating it by smearing Vaseline on it, which was rationed out to us at bedtime to put on our chapped faces. He was able to conceal this rash with the knee-high socks that we wore with our shorts. However, this rash soon developed into a very painful weeping eczema. In hindsight, he was probably an 'atopic' individual, prone to developing allergic dermatitis. I don't know if this tendency continued in his later years or not.

You paint a bleak picture of his early years in school. Was it really all that bad? His letters do not mention any of this.

I am only reporting what I saw. But it might be worth mentioning that the culture of stoicism in boarding schools forbade talking about your woes, for that would have been considered 'weak'. The fact that Kamal was a quiet, sensitive and gentle person would not have helped, for such boys are easily picked on.

However, his circumstances changed in middle school. Or I should say, he changed his circumstances. He developed a thicker hide, an armour of sorts. He started exercising and walked in a somewhat stiff way. With this toughening up, and with the way he carried himself and faced all obstacles, one would think twice before picking a fight with him.

So would you describe Kamal as a strong and silent type?

In a sense, yes. But he certainly did not hold back if he disagreed with something that was said. I will give you an example: In senior school we read both English and Indian history. Unfortunately, the Indian history book was written by a poorly educated Englishman, who wrote, for instance, that Akbar was such a great king that even today Muslims remember him in their prayers, saying 'Allah O Akbar'! Nor did he give an even-handed account of the gradual British 'conquest' of India. Invariably, Indian victories were portrayed as heinous massacres or crimes, and British victories as brave and brilliant against impossible odds. Kamal took strong exception to this portrayal of Indians and spoke out about it to the teacher, something which many of us felt but did not say anything about. Among us, there was never any doubt about Kamal's views and strong character.

Thank you so much for your time. There was one last thing I wanted to ask you. In almost all the group photos of your class over a span of eight years, you and Kamal can be seen standing next to each other. Surely that was more than a coincidence?

In moments like those you tend to congregate with people you know well. In answer to your question, yes, it wasn't just a coincidence. Kamal and I were not only early childhood friends, but also kindred spirits. We understood each other. Though very different in many ways, we shared a certain sensitivity, and we both had a propensity for imagination. The Kamal I knew was a very good, decent and gentle human being. There was also a very appealing upright, emotional honesty to him which led him to take life very seriously. Maybe he was destined to follow the tragic trajectory that his life subsequently took, but he lived as he chose to live. I do not, of course, know what happened at the very end, but I would like to think of him in his last moments flying his Spitfire aircraft fearlessly into the eye of the sun to be invisible to enemy eyes, just like he would pretend to do when we were young boys. Then I imagine his throbbing plane suddenly becoming silent, as it was embraced, at last, in the boundless and peaceful blue of an endless sky.

Thank you, Doctor.

Any time. So, what are you planning to do with all the history you are collecting from so long ago?

For the moment, I am just trying to learn more about the man I never met but heard of often during family gatherings. If I find out enough, I might turn it all into a little book. A memorial of sorts.

1956

After nine months of being away, he is back home for winter vacation. And now he feels like he never left home. He spends hours on end playing with his sisters and teaching them games he has learnt. At bedtime, he tells them stories late into the night: stories about his school, about the haunted graveyard where no one dares to go, about the time a leopard was spotted playing with her cubs and everyone, including the teachers, had to remain indoors after dark for a whole week until the police sent the leopard family packing. His sisters listen to every word he says with rapt attention and ask him to fill in missing bits. 'What did the policemen do to the leopard family?' asks one sister. 'What games were the cubs playing?' asks the other.

When his sisters are off at school and it is just him and his mother in the house, he follows her around and questions her incessantly about everything she has been up to during his absence. '*Ufff*—how do you expect me to remember all those details?' is his mother's refrain. But the person he yearns for most is the person he sees the least—his father, who is posted to a remote military outpost where families cannot visit. Occasionally, and unexpectedly, his father comes home for a weekend, rarely longer. On those rare visits, he basks in his father's presence.

And so the winter passes, much faster than he would like, and it is only towards its end, when it is time for him to return to school, that melancholy overcomes him. When it is time to collect his new clothes from the tailor—Rexona Darzi—he accompanies his mother to the market in silence. His mother's words of consolation, '*Itna udaas mat ho* . . . I will visit you in the summer,' fail to lift his spirits.

o o o

For coming first in class during the previous academic year, he has been told to head over to the school library to pick any one of the new books of his choosing; the book he selects will be wrapped and awarded to him ceremoniously at the upcoming Founder's Day.

After careful deliberation, he selects a photo-filled encyclopaedia of plants, in keeping with his budding interest in botany. The main draw of the book for him, however, are the little packets of seeds taped inside the back cover, and instructions on how to plant them. The prospect of planting his own little garden delights him. Once he has the book in hand, his plan is to find a suitable plot of land that is secluded enough so his plants will not be trampled upon.

Kamal (aged ten) holding the book awarded to him for coming at the top of his class. He was a regular recipient of many such awards during his years in school.

○ ○ ○

Sometimes he feels besieged, for the entire world, or almost all of it, seems to be conspiring against him. First, there is the matter of getting vaccinated twice. During the winter vacation, his mother had made sure all his vaccinations were up to date and had handed him a certificate as proof; he was to present it to the school authorities when asked, but he had misplaced it. Before he could explain himself to the nurse, he had been given another jab in the arm. He knows his mother will be upset when she finds out, and he has been bracing himself for the letter he expects from her any day now.

His mother's reaction, however, is only the smaller of his worries. He is more bothered by two boys who have ganged up against him and have started to needlessly torment him. Why they pick on him, he does not know, but they are making his life utterly miserable. Their latest mischief is hiding his belongings: just the previous day it was his shoes that went missing. It had taken him a long time to find them inside the dustbin, which in turn had made him late for study hour and had resulted in a scolding from the housemaster.

Fortunately, not everything in his life is gloomy, for now he has not one, not two, but six close friends—Arora, Dhillon, Obi, Shahid, Joshi and Vikram. In a letter to his mother, he reports that his *'pukkey dost'* help him look for his belongings if they go missing or end up in the dustbin mysteriously.

There has been another positive development in his life—he has landed a role in the end-of-year junior school play.[i] Casting calls for *Snow White and the Seven Dwarves* had been announced some days earlier and he had promptly thrown his name into the hat. At the audition, he had been asked to read a passage from the script and he had done it with a flourish: he had raised

---

[i] The senior school play that year was called *The Happiest Days of Your Life* and the leading role was played by a boy named Amitabh Bachchan.

his voice, enunciated his words, even used his hands for emphasis. In the end, his efforts had paid off and he had been given the role of one of the dwarves, although he suspects his short stature might also have played a role in him landing the part. Nevertheless, his is a key part in the play and in a letter to his parents, he reports that it requires him to memorize exactly four full pages worth of script. He also reports that he rehearses his lines daily for he intends to act well in the play.

One arena where his below-average height does not help him is sports. On the track he gives his all, but it is never enough to beat his longer-limbed classmates. In the gymnasium, he can barely touch the parallel bars with outstretched arms and the instructor has to raise him so he can latch on to the apparatus and get started with his routine. But he enjoys sports too much to let these shortcomings hold him back. And whatever he lacks in size, he more than makes up for with heart. In every sport he plays, he plays his heart out. At a recent soccer match, he was singled out for his perseverance: when an opponent got possession of the ball, he gave chase the entire length of the field, over and over again. As a result, his classmates have started calling him 'Bulldog' for his tenaciousness, and try to get him on their team, more for his spunk than his talent.

However, his favourite sport by far, now, is boxing. He loves putting his nerves to the test, loves parrying his opponent's punches, loves plotting a quick counter-attack when possible. To his satisfaction, he has been getting rather good at it all. In the recent boxing tournament, he won his first bout against Charlie and the second one against Bose. His victory run ended thereafter, in his third bout against Mehta, when he found himself on the back foot more often than not, dodging more jabs than he was landing. He had been disappointed with his loss and had reflected on it for days afterwards, wondering what he could have done differently to counter Mehta's barrages. He has some ideas that he intends to try next time around.

1957

Madsen, a boy from the sixth standard, has just swum a hundred laps of the newly built swimming pool and is still at it. All the boys are cheering Madsen, but not him as he is in shock. How can Madsen, who is barely a year older than him, swim so great a distance, while he cannot even traverse the width of the pool?

It is not from a lack of trying that he is unable to swim. Ever since the pool opened a month ago, he has been coming for practice almost daily and with full concentration has been following the instructor's directions on how to move his arms and kick his legs. But nothing has helped so far. After pushing off from the side of the pool, he splashes around and then down he goes. His lack of progress pains him even more when he watches the few boys who can swim plunge

joyfully into the deep end and effortlessly stay afloat.
He yearns to be like them.

It is after completing a hundred and four laps—a
new school record—that Madsen finally steps out of
the pool to cheers from all present. As for him, he
cannot imagine anyone in the school ever breaking
that record. 'Perhaps Madsen will break his own record
someday,' he writes in his letter to his parents.

○○○

It is the annual Founder's Day and once again he is
marching up to the podium to collect a prize, this time
for coming first in English. The book that he had
chosen for his prize is titled *Card Conjuring* by Wilfrid
Jonson. It describes how one can use sleight of hand to
perform magic tricks with a deck of cards.

His interest in conjuring took hold when the
school invited a magician for a show. Over the
better part of an hour, the magician had performed a
range of tricks, making things magically appear and
disappear. Throughout the show, he had watched the
magician's hands with rapt attention to understand
how the magician did that, but he had come up empty;
however keen his eyes, they were no match for the
deftness of the magician. For days after the show, he
had wondered how the magician had performed those
tricks. And then, just by chance, when he had been
called to the library to select a book for his prize, he

had spotted Wilfrid Jonson's book. He was thrilled, and had selected it right away for his prize.

Now, as he walks back to his seat among the prize winners, he can't wait to get to the bottom of at least some of the magician's many secrets.

◦◦◦

It is easily the worst birthday of his life as he is bedridden with a high fever and a nasty cough. And he is not alone—over half the school is down with the same flu.[1]

Exactly how the virus made its way to Indian shores, and eventually to his school, is hard to retrace, but the generally accepted theory is that it came via Singapore aboard the passenger ship *SS Rajula*. At least forty-four passengers on board the ship were known to have developed flu-like symptoms before it made landfall in Madras. In spite of all the precautions taken by the authorities in quarantining the sick, the virus had still spread among the local residents and then had fanned out across the country over the following weeks. In mid-July—a week before his birthday—it reached his school. So many had fallen sick so quickly that the school infirmary had been inundated, and the main auditorium, Milman Hall, had also been turned into a temporary ward.

As for him, he is none too pleased with the timing of the flu's onset. For his birthday celebration, he had planned on treating his friends to a movie in town followed by cake, but all those plans had to be abandoned now. Worse still, the flu had resulted in the closure of the swimming pool just when he had improved his swimming technique to the point where he could traverse the length of the pool. Although his personal record of one lap is a far cry from Madsen's 104, he is nonetheless pleased with it and intends to do better as soon as he is permitted back in the water.

Kamal (aged eleven) demonstrating his swimming technique
to his sisters Kiki and Niki.

○○○

It is almost three in the morning, and he is being roused by the teacher accompanying the schoolboys on their train journey home for vacation. 'Your stop is next,' the teacher informs him.

On the platform of Ambala Cantonment railway station, he spots his mother and aunt Kanta before they see him. His sisters had insisted on coming along too, his mother explains, but their valiant effort at staying awake past midnight had failed. His father could not come as he had already headed off to his new posting.

Sensing his disappointment, his mother reassures him that the family will be reunited soon; the plan is for them to join his father where his newest posting has taken him, as soon as he can find a suitable house for them.

○ ○ ○

The one thing that truly excites him about living in Ambala is that an Indian Air Force squadron is stationed there, and so fighter aircraft can be seen flying overhead. On some days, he cycles over to the airfield and sets himself down by the perimeter fence for a closer look at the aircraft taking off. It is something he can do for hours on end—watch aircraft lift into the sky and disappear into the clouds beyond as the drone of their engines grows fainter. Sometimes, he even catches sight of sleek silver-coloured fighter jets that are starting to replace the older propeller planes. He tries to imagine what it must be like sitting in one of them. He sure would like to find out some day.

At other times, when he is not spotting airplanes or dreaming of them, he accompanies his mother on her various errands to prepare for moving homes. Much needs to be done: thick *razais* need to be sewn because the cantonment they are moving to is located in the hills and nights are going to be chilly; fabric needs to be selected, bought and handed over to Rexona Darzi for stitching a blazer, two pairs of trousers and three sets of night suits for him, and skirts and shirts for his sisters; new sarees need to be selected from Peshawar Cloth House for his mother, for when she attends dinner parties with his father at the officers' mess. It is on Christmas Day that his mother finally gives the all-clear for the move, and sends word ahead to his father of their arrival two days later.

To get to Dagshai, and their new home, they first take a train to Kalka, then a bus to Dharampur, doing the last leg to Dagshai in a 1-ton truck that his father has arranged for them. He is excited by the trip and the adventure of the various modes of transportation.

The house his father has rented is as charming as the drive up to it. It is a bungalow with a large bay window at the far end, overlooking snow-capped mountains to the east and the Indian plains to the west. When night falls, his father points out the shimmering lights of the new city of Chandigarh in the plains below.

He is happy: happy to be living in such a beautiful setting, happy knowing that when he awakens the next morning, and on the many mornings to follow, his entire family will be present with him, all under the same roof—being with his family is what he treasures most.

Kamal (aged eleven) back home for winter vacation.

Kiki and Niki

(Kiki Bakshi is an educator and life coach, based in Canada. She is Kamal's younger sister.

Niki Kumar is a former administrator at the Department of Social Security in the UK. She is Kamal's youngest sister.)

[Author] *Mrs Bakshi and Mrs Kumar, because Dagshai features prominently in your brother's story, I decided to pay it a visit. I see why it held a special place in his heart. It sure is beautiful up there. I was wondering if you could give me a glimpse into your lives there in the late fifties.*

[K and N] Dagshai was one of our fondest postings. We lived in a lovely bungalow there. At some point long ago, it used to be a Masonic Lodge, and because of the secretive ways of the Freemasons that none of the locals understood, people started referring to the house as '*Jadoo Ghar*'. It sure was magical for us, although in a different way. So high up on the mountain were we that clouds and mist would drift into our bedroom through open windows. I remember my mother rushing around the house ordering us to shut the windows when this happened, or else our bed linen would get damp from the moisture.

During the day we were, of course, busy with schoolwork, but in the evenings, we would walk down to the town centre to meet our friends. All the kids gathered there because of a wonderful store located there. It was called the Army-Navy Store and the proprietor was a man named Babulal. All of us kids would bring pocket money to buy treats. Bull's eyes sweets were our favourite!

I did go down to that store and met Babulal there . . .

Really? My goodness! Babulal must be over a hundred years old now. He was a grown man when I was a child almost sixty years ago. How was he?

He looked great. He remembered your father. In fact, he was the one who gave me directions to your house.

That is incredible. It must be the fresh mountain air that is keeping him going.

It was an idyllic life we lived there: sheltered in the safety and beauty of a pretty little army town with pleasant weather. It was a far cry from the heat and chaos that is common across Indian cities.

Your mother's diary has an entry saying that your father had to leave suddenly for Delhi, something about him having to accompany a visiting Chinese delegation?

Our father spoke Mandarin Chinese fluently, so he was one of the translator-cum-liaison officers designated to accompany a visiting Chinese military delegation, led by Marshal Ye Jianying, as they toured across India.

Your brother must have been very disappointed with your father having to leave?

Why do you say that? I remember us feeling proud about the appointment; it was a big deal that he was being asked to guide the Chinese delegation. He sent picture postcards to each of us, separately, from every city he went to.

As per my notes, your father left for Delhi a couple of weeks after your brother returned home for vacation. By my calculation, your brother got to spend exactly three weeks with his father over a period of two years. That must have disappointed your brother, considering how much he yearned to spend time with his father.

That leads me to my next question: What was their relationship like? What did they do on the rare occasions they were together?

Please recheck your math! Three weeks over two years cannot be correct. Plus, you did not count the times our father visited our brother in school. An Army officer gets two whole months of leave each year and many days of casual leave.

As for how they spent their time together—both loved the outdoors. They would go exploring. They often discussed how a person could live off the land when out in the wilderness. That reminds me—my father and my brother loved reading books by Jim Corbett, the naturalist. Between them, they had all of Corbett's books.

(*Laughing*) I just remembered another story of my father and brother's adventures. In this case, it was a misadventure. One time, the two of them decided to give fishing a try. But it was a disaster. My mother complained about how much money my father had spent on buying an expensive fishing rod and all the accoutrements, and then the two of them returned home empty-handed. For a long time afterwards, my mother would tease them: '*Koi machhli nahi pakdi,*' she would say.

Could you jog back your memories to the winter months when your brother would come home on vacation?

Our brother would come home for three months each year: from December through February.

Thanks to him, those were our most cherished months of the year. He was just so full of life and our days would simply fly by when he was around. He would play with us, amuse us, tell us all sorts of stories from school, teach us new games and card tricks and naughty rhymes that he would spontaneously make up. He even taught us how to dance. Back in those days, there used to be a programme on Radio Ceylon called the *Binaca Hit Parade*. They would play the most popular songs of the day. He would dance his heart out, and we would follow him.

Another time he started writing a family newspaper to report on the goings-on at home. He called the newspaper 'The Canning Notifier' as, by then, we had moved to Ambala and lived at 28 Canning Road. In this newspaper, he would report on picnics and outings we went on, descriptions and details of dinner parties thrown by our parents; in one he interviewed our aunt Kanta about a sweater she was knitting for our father. It was a very detailed interview— he asked her how she went about making the stitches, why she had selected the colours that she had, etc.

In your mother's diary from that time, she often mentions a man named Santokh Singh. Your brother

*too, in his letters home, mentions a Santokh Singh
ji. Who was he?*

Santokh Singh ji was our father's batman. He
was an extremely impressive man: dignified,
polite, dependable, loyal. As a batman, his job
was to support our father with his military work,
but being the kind of man he was, he quickly
won us all over. Especially our brother. In fact,
he was a sort of mentor to our brother. I did not
know the two of them exchanged letters, but
I am not surprised that they did.

*As you know, your brother thought highly of Sikh
soldiers. Could Santokh Singh have been the reason
for it?*

Hmm . . . that is an interesting observation. It
is possible. My brother was at an impressionable
age at that point, and Santokh Singh was a man
of impeccable character; the sort of person my
brother was drawn to, then and later in life. So it
is definitely possible. In fact, there was one other
solider—also a Sikh—who was just as impressive
and whom we all dearly loved. His name was
Kundan Singh. It is likely the two played a large
role in my brother having a favourable opinion
of Sikh soldiers.

1958

Flying is all he thinks about nowadays. It had started out as any schoolboy's fantasy but now has turned into a full-blown obsession of his. In the school library, he hunts down all the books on aircraft and reads them from cover to cover, and then reads them again. On the margins of his notebooks, and in his letters home, he sketches scenes of air battles. His teachers have started to take note too: in the end-of-month academic report that gets mailed to his parents, his English composition teacher complains, 'He writes beautifully and has developed a writing style that is uniquely his own. But he turns every writing assignment into a WW2 flying adventure.'

Rasam

(Colonel Rasam Chand Katoch is a retired Army officer. He was Kamal's classmate in school and batchmate in the National Defence Academy.)

[Author] *Sir, you were among Kamal's closest friends in school. Do you remember his obsession with airplanes?*

[R] Of course. Kamal loved everything to do with flying and planes—building them, drawing them, reading about them. He was especially fond of reading the Biggles flying adventure books by Capt. W.E. Johns; he strongly identified with the main character, Wing Commander Biggles, who valiantly and single-handedly overcame all misfortunes and disasters that came his way. In fact, his obsession with the Biggles books earned him the nickname 'Commander'; it stuck with him for the remainder of our time in school. He also started drawing airplanes, initially Spitfires—Biggles' plane—but this interest soon extended to all kinds of planes.

He also became very fond of playing games that involved pretending he was flying planes and shooting down the enemy. He would hide in trees and jump down on a passer-by as though he were a fighter ace diving down on his prey.

In my autograph book, as far back as 1959, when he was barely thirteen, he wrote a note saying he had decided to join the air force.

The first time Kamal mentioned you in his letters was in August 1958, although not your name specifically. He wrote 'My best friend won the boxing championship' and after cross-referencing the school magazine from that year, I realized he was referring to you. As per the blurb in the school magazine, it was an epic fight between you and your opponent. Do you remember that day?

Yes, of course. One does not forget such moments in one's life. It was a long and tough match. And I won it.

Do you recall how his match went? I know he did not make it to the championship round that year.

No, I do not recall his match. But I can tell you that he was a fearless fighter.

I heard the same thing from another boxer named Joshi who was a batch junior to yours. He too said that Kamal was a spirited fighter and that the boxing coach, Mr Miller, was very fond of him.

*Before we close, sir, I wanted to ask you, if I may—
what was it about Kamal that drew you to him as
a friend?*

There was not just one thing; it was many little
things about him that all added up to what he
was. Starting with his personality. I can tell you
that Kamal had grit. He never gave up. He was
just so resilient and determined.

Another quality of his was his sense of
adventure. He loved going for walks in the hills
around our school. One time, he came across a
spot with caves and made himself a hideaway
camp there. If I could not find him in school, I
knew he must have gone to his secret spot.

His adventurous streak remained with him
into his adult life. Once I told him about a
tough-to-climb mountain near my ancestral
village in Himachal Pradesh. Sometime after
that, Kamal headed up to my village, stayed
with my parents for a night and then scaled
that same mountain all by himself. Such was his
spirit. Another thing about Kamal that comes to
mind was his curiosity about everything. During
our long hikes in the hills around Nainital, he
would demonstrate incredible knowledge of the
trees and plants we came across. That reminds
me: in general knowledge tests, Kamal was

usually the top person in school. And yet, even though he was bright and fearless and tough, he was not arrogant. There was a down-to-earth humility about him which I admired.

I must tell you that the admiration was mutual. In a letter that Kamal wrote to one of his sisters almost ten years after you both became friends, he said that among all the men he knew, there were only two that were worthy of being called gentlemen. You were one of the two.

[No response]

1959

In celebration of the school nurse, Mrs Johnson, giving birth to her first child, the school has declared a holiday; students are free to do what they want. With all lessons cancelled, his class teacher offers to take whoever is interested for a walk in the woods. He takes up the teacher's offer right away.

He enjoys these walks among the pines, the deodars and the chestnut trees that border his school, especially the part when the teacher points out a tree or a plant and quizzes the boys about it. Invariably, it is he who replies with the correct answer. Sometimes, he adds additional details that he thinks might be of interest to the teacher: 'This plant can also cure indigestion, and that one over there is an antidote for skin rash,' he adds.

When they return to school, the teacher invites the boys to his quarters for refreshments and plays a record of a pipe band on his gramophone. Soon, the plaintive sounds of bagpipes fill the room.

It is not the first time he is hearing pipes being played—his father's regiment has a pipe band and he has often heard them play marching tunes. But the beauty of the melodies he hears now moves him deeply and leaves an indelible impression on him. He does not know it yet, but years from now, he too will be an accomplished bagpiper.

○○○

He is walking out of the school gates with a bounce in his step and his head held high, for he is among a select few who have been permitted to go out to town for the weekend; the rest are staying put on campus.

His being a part of this special group had come about the day before when the swimming coach had presented his class with a challenge: only boys who can dive off the highest diving platform without killing themselves would be allowed to go to town on the upcoming weekend. A handful of his classmates had taken up the coach's challenge right away, but most had lacked the courage, including him. Even though he was a confident swimmer now and did not think twice before somersaulting into the deep end, the top platform was an altogether different beast. So small did everything appear from up there that it seemed to him he might miss the swimming pool entirely if he leapt too far. But no matter how hard he tried, he could not ignore the challenge; he knew that the thought that he lacked the guts to do this would gnaw away at him later. The following day, he marched right up to the top and slew the monster.

1962

For the past month, he has been glued to the wireless set to listen to news reports of the Chinese invasion of Ladakh and North-East Frontier Agency (NEFA), and each morning the news gets worse: Indian forces keep getting pushed back by the advancing Chinese. And today's bulletin is the worst so far, with the Prime Minister himself coming on air to announce that the Chinese have broken through Se La Pass, putting them within striking distance of the Indian plains!

The news breaks his heart. He wants to do something. Anything. Perhaps he should rush off to the border to help in any way he can, knowing fully well that he will be stopped way before he gets anywhere near there. His consolation lies in knowing that he is about to do his part for the country—he

has already been accepted at the National Defence
Academy in Khadakvasla and will be heading there in
a little over two months to begin his military training.
Once he earns his wings—he intends to pick the Air
Force as his service of choice—he will do everything
in his power to ensure the country never retreats in
battle, certainly not on his watch.

Ian

(Ian Atkinson is a television producer and writer based in Australia. He was Kamal's classmate in school.)

[Author] *Mr Atkinson, thank you for agreeing to answer some questions about your classmate Kamal.*

[I] Please call me Ian. You can drop the Mister.

Very well, Ian. To start off, I wanted to ask you what words come to mind if you had to describe Kamal to someone who did not know him.

Someone who was extremely bright. And extremely driven. Someone who knew his mind. Someone who had a presence. A strong presence.

And what was it about him that made you choose him as a friend?

Please understand that you did not make Kamal your friend. No—he decided who his friends were going to be! And once his friend, you were lavished with loyalty, consideration and his full attention. That is how he was.

In my early years in school, I just knew him in passing. Although we were in the same class, we were in different houses and so, competed against each other in sports. And we had different interests—I liked swimming and girls, while he was a boxer and took his studies seriously. So our paths rarely crossed. But in our final year in school in '62, both of us were appointed school monitors. As a perk of being monitors, we were given our own private rooms. Tiny though they were, yet they were large enough to accommodate a bed, a cupboard and a desk. We also had a window each looking out towards the snow-covered Himalayas. Our rooms abutted and were separated by a thin plywood panel so we could talk to each other through it.

Both of us shared a love for flying. We would make little airplanes that we would launch from the top of the school building and would watch them sail down to the valley below. One of our airplanes made it really far. We were sure we set a world record with that one, but we did not have a witness to our claim. Kamal was also among the world's best WW2 military aircraft drawers and proudly displayed his works of art on his cupboard. He had a beautiful and detailed drawing of an aircraft banking into a turn in the skies above England.

That reminds me of another incident: Something I loved doing at night back then was playing my guitar and singing. At first, I was worried that my terrible playing would disturb the studious guy next door so I would sing softly, until one day Kamal yelled out, 'Ian *yaar*—let your voice come out!' And so I did, and I could hear him drumming and humming in the background next door . . . and making corrections to my lyrics! Our close friendship grew from there, out of mutual respect for one another's different abilities. He was really good at getting people to overcome shyness or doubts. You kind of felt that with Kamal, all you had to do was try and you had his support. He never judged you badly if you didn't quite do what you thought you could. I also admired the way he was able to discipline himself to anything he set his mind to do.

As for what he found admirable about me, I can only speculate. Other than writing poetry, I could not spend time 'internalizing' stuff. I think that's when Kamal decided that he would make me his friend. I think he saw the internal struggle I had with taking study seriously and he saw that I had a gift for expressing myself in verse and song. So, I think, initially, I might have become one of his projects! I certainly responded to the nice way he had of encouraging my literary efforts.

I have a question about his temperament. Some people I have spoken to remember him as being quiet and studious. Some said he could be found either walking in the woods or sitting in the school library. That gives me the impression of him being introverted. Is that how he was?

I can understand why some would have interpreted his love of reading and study as 'introverted'. Nothing could be further from the truth. Kamal had what the French so beautifully call *joie de vivre*, a 'love of life'. His enthusiasm and energy were infectious. And he had a forceful character.

I can give you one example of that: According to Kamal, I was the best-looking guy in school. I am telling you this not to toot my own horn, but to give you an example of Kamal's character. Now Kamal's claim was hotly disputed by our friends Mandeep and Sanjay, who rooted for our classmate Kabir Bedi.[ii] But Kamal was such a fierce and feisty warrior who just said things like they were a long-established fact. And you did not argue with Kamal unless you knew for sure that you

---

[ii] Kabir Bedi would go on to become a successful film actor in India and abroad. He would also play the villain in a James Bond production called *Octopussy*.

would win; he was a brainy fellow and chances were that he knew something that you did not. Imagine what it was like to have an ally like that.

If you want the essence of his personality, think of a man who loved looking at the mountains and the stars while his mind freewheeled, discovering new ways to understand everyday things. I am sure the only reason he spent so much time reading was to find out if someone else had already thought of the same things as him. And underlying his creative free spirit was the strongest sense of discipline and responsibility to his parents and teachers. Both of us had fathers in the military and for both of us, the most important thing in life was to have a solid sense of personal honour. Kamal had that . . . big time.

3

Youth
1963–1967

Kiki

[Author] *Mrs Bakshi, I must say I find your brother a bit of an enigma. Some of his friends describe him as reserved, while others describe him as outgoing. Some describe him as the studious type who would often be seen in the library, while others describe him as a keen sportsman.*

[K] It is all true. My brother was indeed all of that. He was always up to something, always kept himself busy, always had a project he would be working on to improve himself or to learn something new. But even though he often kept to himself, he was very extroverted as well. In the evenings when our friends dropped in, my brother was at the centre of all the fun. Led by him, we would play all sorts of games. He was the one who taught me and all my friends how to dance.

I see. A person of very contrasting temperaments, your brother was. Getting back to the winter of 1962: your brother was sixteen years old then, a vigorous young lad in the prime of his youth. Did he ever tell you about any romantic involvements he might have had around then?

He told us everything. Everything. In fact, his first crush was at age fifteen, and then a second, more serious one when he was sixteen.

This girl, his serious crush, who was she?

(*Laughing*) If you are looking for a name, you will not get it from me. You should just stick to the facts about his life.

This is an important fact of his life. A first kiss is a turning point in anyone's life—is it not?

[No response]

Ok—let us skip names. But please do tell what the girl was like.

Bright-eyed. Quick-witted. Delicate-featured. She had a lovely voice and laughter to match. She was always smiling; a very sweet person.

And then what happened?

Nothing. He headed off to the NDA. And her Army dad got posted elsewhere.

That's it?

Yes, that is it.

Hmmm . . . Okay. Was there anyone else in his life? Someone he mentioned in passing, perhaps?

Yes, there was. A girl from Sikkim. My brother told me about her a few months before the war. He said he was very close to her.

I want to meet this person. Can you please put me in touch with her? I promise not to intrude on her personal life; I just want her to help me understand your brother better. That is all.

I honestly know nothing about her. Nor did I ever meet her, and so I cannot even describe her to you. All I know is that she was Sikkimese. I too wish very much that I had met her, or could meet her now!

1963

He has been in the National Defence Academy for barely a few months and has already gained a reputation for being unconventional. An example: during a recent lecture, the topic of discussion had been the role of an officer in a military unit. While some had described an officer as one who must instil order and discipline and whatnot among his men, his views were thus:

> Just as a mother nurtures her children, so must a good officer nurture his fighting men. Just as a

mother shields her children from unnecessary risks, so must an officer. And, just as a good mother parents with humility, so must an officer. Any officer worth half his salt must do all these things to be able to live up to the trust that his men put in him. But to be fully worth his salt, he must be many times better. He must be a demi-god in the eyes of his men, not an ordinary man. And to do that, he must live like a demi-god: with integrity and majesty and honour.

His comments had resulted in raised eyebrows and glances exchanged. It would not be the last time this would be the reaction to his opinions.

○ ○ ○

It is Sunday, and he is in a cinema hall watching a western called *Sergeants 3*. Inevitably, a fight breaks out between army cavalrymen and the natives, and predictably, it is the armed soldiers who get the better of the natives. After the film, he makes his way back to the Academy and mulls over the parts that he enjoyed most, which happens to be every scene depicting the natives. Their demeanour and vigour and courage— they fight with knives and tomahawks, knowing fully well they are no match for rifles—make a deep impression on him.

The following day, he heads down to the library in search of books describing life on America's frontiers and finds two: *The Last of the Mohicans* by James

Fenimore Cooper and *The Oregon Trail* by Francis
Packman. He reads them with deep interest, paying
particular attention to passages that describe native
lifestyle: their spartan homes, raw food diet, living
off the land sustainably, hunting only for sustenance
and never for sport, and using every part of their kill.
In his diary entry, he notes that 'from one bear an
Injun[1] gets meat for nourishment, hide for clothing,
sinews for rope making, bones for forming spearheads
and enough fat for cooking year around'. Over the
following days, he dwells on the native way of living
and summarizes his thoughts in a mini treatise thus:

> An Injun is one who has vitality in every action—
> in his posture, position of biceps and triceps and
> dynamically tense chest and shoulders. When he
> drinks water, he lets each gulp go down vitally,
> knowingly and in a controlled manner into his
> stomach. When he breathes, he breathes deeply.
> When performing any action, from physical feats
> to merely stepping across two paces, he does it with
> deep vitality. This vitality, in form and action, each
> moment of one's life, is the secret of the Indian
> spirit.

Thereon, he decides he will make Injun warriors
his role models. Like them, he too will be bold in his
conduct, savage in battle, and will live life in a spartan
manner.

1964

It is starting to get dark as he makes his way back to the academy after taking a long solitary walk in the woods around Khadakvasla and he is in a state of rapture. He records his thoughts in his diary later that night:

> An experience which will be a way of life for me was felt. I romped over the dusk-fresh countryside, walking, and prancing out of sheer joy and deer agility. I leapt and manoeuvred over my path and gave myself up to the loving hands of nature. I stood and breathed in the evening wind and let it caress me. I watched quail burst up and down the hillside and I felt a real son of the wild. I believe the secret to good health, and agelessness right until death, is to give oneself to nature.
>
> I must 'live' as much as I can in the great outdoors; this will cure me fully, and my eyesight. I can do so a minimum four times a week— Wednesdays, Saturday evenings and Sunday morning and evenings; also, on some working days and holidays and on all opportunities. And when briefly indoors, I must live in a spartan outdoor manner, reflecting the wild's movements in every action, in every breath; I must make it a full part of me.

oOo

That he is erudite is not disputed by anyone—his answers are well-received by class instructors and he is often seen in the library with a stack of books on whatever new subject has caught his fancy. And so it comes as a surprise to everyone when the year-end examination results are posted on the notice board. All can see that he has failed. As a result, not only will he have to repeat the academic term, he will also have to address his coursemates as 'sir', for they will gain seniority over him over the entirety of his military career. When asked by acquaintances as to why he failed to advance to the next course, he only says that he did not hit the books hard enough.

Rasam

[Author] *Colonel, an Army officer told me that Kamal got relegated to a junior batch while in the NDA, but the officer did not know why. Since you were among Kamal's closest friends, I was wondering if Kamal told you the reason.*

[R] He did tell me, but only after I asked him point-blank what was going on. He said it was because his eyesight was not up to Air Force requirements. You see, after completing two years of general training at the NDA, the cadets receive further training in their chosen service—Army, Air Force or Navy. But Air Force cadets have to go through a special medical examination where their eyesight is checked.

So why flunk his exams?

To buy himself time to improve his eyesight. Kamal, being Kamal, was not going to just sit back and take whatever fate threw his way. He went around looking for a solution and found a book[2] by some doctor who claimed that eyesight could be improved by doing eye exercises. And unknown to everyone, that is what Kamal had done every day for two years. But it had not worked.

Shortly before our second-year exams, he had his eyes checked and found out that his vision had not improved. And what does Kamal do on finding out that his efforts for the past two years have not paid off? He decides he needs to try harder and so he flunks out to buy himself more time. And that was not the end of it. When the next examinations rolled around, he got his eyesight tested again. Once again it was not up to snuff. So he flunked again!

A double relegation?

Yes! The two of us joined NDA in the twenty-ninth course, but he graduated with the thirty-first course. The only reason he did not flunk a third time was because he would have been expelled from the academy.

1965

It is night-time and he is sitting at his desk, planning out his life if he is forced to leave the academy. Something he is absolutely sure about is that he intends to live a life filled with adventure and being outdoors. After some thought, he draws up a list of three professions that he could transition to: forest management, tea plantation management and journalism. However, none of these professions are to be an end in itself for him, but rather a means to reach his greater goal of venturing out on his own. Once he can save Rs 10,000, he plans to buy some acreage in the hills. In one corner of his land, he will build himself a log house out of pine; the rest he will cultivate. In the evenings, when he is done tending to the holding, he will sit at his writing desk, compile all the adventures offered by country living and submit them for publication. As for the delicate matter of finding a suitable mate, he will take his time and remain a bachelor for as long as it takes to find a girl who shares his interests. And if he does find her, he will win her over with the plan that he has already thought out: he will appreciate what she says; compliment her; treat her like a lady; never will he try to show her how big a shot he his, or act the fashionable type. Instead, he would introduce her to his adventurous lifestyle, which they would share.

∘ ∘ ∘

He has arrived at a decision—he is going to shelve his plans for joining the Air Force; he will remain in the Academy and will switch to the Army as his service of choice.

1966

It is the day of his graduation from NDA. To mark the occasion, the junior cadets are doing a march-past for him and his fellow graduates. After the procession ends, the guest of honour, the President of India, Sarvepalli Radhakrishnan, will give a speech and then present awards to the graduates for their accomplishments over the past year. He will be bagging quite a few of those awards, as he reports in a letter to one of his sisters:

Dear Kikiji,

Thank you very much for your letter and tikka. It arrived pat on time.

I hope you managed to attend that party after all, and that it was fun. Did you just hobnob with others in polite and meaningless conversation, or were you better off at the end of it than before it?

Over here it can be said mainly that we are sitting twiddling our thumbs in wait for the end of term festivities, at which we passing out course will be guests, for a change. The President will take the P.O.P. (passing out parade) salute, and the Academy is being scrubbed and repainted to give him a good impression. The Supreme Commander, remember.

Can a bit of khubber intrude in your letter for mummy daddy too? That being that I have done particularly well in academics this time, missing coming first in English by one mark (I got 62, the first man 63). Current policy may give me a second prize. If a commendation carries through, I will also get a prize in History for the most advanced knowledge and biggest mark average. In Chinese I had the highest tally of 65. In practical map reading I had the highest marks and adding the theory marks I have come first in Map Reading in the course. I should not have described this little doing at length, but for a total failure (last year) a chance such as this, to wallow briefly in a penny worth of achievement, comes rarely.

Your loving brother,

Kamal

Undated photo of Kamal with his parents in Tezpur, Assam.

1967

There is a solitary figure running laps around the athletic track of the Indian Military Academy (IMA), Dehradun. It is him. Again. As to why he has been singled out for punishment, he is not entirely sure. All he knows is that his answer did not go down well with a senior officer. Again.

IJS

(Lt. Colonel Inderjeet Singh is a retired Army officer and the former dean of the Chitkara School of Planning and Architecture. He was with Kamal at the Indian Military Academy, Dehradun.)

[Author] *Colonel, you said you often saw Kamal being singled out for extra drills as punishment. Do you have any recollection as to what he might have said that kept landing him in hot water again and again?*

[IJS] I do not recall anything in particular. But I can tell you that Kamal was not a 'yes man'. He spoke his mind without holding back, no matter whom he was speaking with. Some senior officers appreciate such honesty, but unfortunately some do not.

I see. Is that what drew you to him? His honesty?

That. And his persona.

How would you describe his persona? What words come to mind when you think back to the man you met on your first day in IMA in 1967 and became close friends with?

Let's see . . .

He was extremely tenacious: if he set himself a goal, he went all the way trying to achieve it.

He was an avid reader: he would read all the time, about everything under the sun, so conversing with him was always interesting.

And he was also a dreamer: he showed me designs of an aircraft he was working on. He planned to build it all by himself when he had saved up enough.

You mean a radio-controlled airplane?

No, an actual aircraft that a person could fly themselves.

Interesting! Please continue . . .

He was also a fitness fanatic: he would punish himself physically, over and over again. One time, he walked from Ambala train station to my house in Chandigarh because he did not want to wait around for a bus. The next day he walked from Chandigarh to Shimla because there were three of us and my scooter could only carry two up the hills.

I also remember the time he returned from the Chindits[3] exercise. It is the toughest exercise a GC (Gentleman Cadet) undertakes in the

IMA before getting commissioned as an officer. One must spend a week in the wilderness, survive extremely tough conditions, then complete the exercise with a 50-km run back to the Academy carrying a heavy load and a weapon. Being a term junior to him, I was waiting for him at the Military Academy gates to welcome him back, and recall seeing that he was in bad shape and running a high fever. It turned out that a cadet in Kamal's company had been hurt and it had fallen upon Kamal to carry the injured man's backpack. It is brutal enough carrying one's own load; carrying a second pack on Chindits is unimaginable. And yet, he had done it.

Now when I think back to him, I would describe Kamal as being like a Van Gogh painting: bold, colourful, exciting, and yet with a touch of irony.

Thank you so very much, Colonel. One last thing—I wanted to tell you that Kamal mentioned you in a letter he wrote in 1969, addressed to one of his sisters who was a college student at the time. This is what he wrote:

> '. . . *By the way, you are not to go out with anyone calling himself a friend of mine, in or out of*

> *uniform. I write this because one or two blighters are visiting Chandigarh and they don't muster half a gentleman among them. No one I know is fit enough to associate with you, or any of your friends for that matter, except let's say RCK and IJS.'*
>
> He obviously thought highly of you, Colonel.
>
> [No response]

December

He is dressing up in formals for it is his special day—the day he gets commissioned as a military officer. After buttoning up his coat and slipping on his 'shoulder titles', to cover his epaulettes for the ceremony later, he heads out to the assembly area.

Kiki

[Author] *Mrs Bakshi, what are your recollections from the day your brother was commissioned as an Army officer?*

[K] Oh, I remember everything! It was my mother and I who had gone to attend his commissioning. We got all dressed up in special sarees for the functions at the IMA. My mother was especially happy and proud, now that both her husband and son were Army officers.

I remember a lovely ritual they have at IMA after the swearing-in ceremony. Everyone gathers in the banquet hall. The young men are in full uniform, but their epaulette flaps are still covered with the old shoulder titles they wore as gentlemen cadets. These are grey and maroon circular bands of fabric, that now conceal the new insignia. The banquet hall lights are switched off briefly, and in the pitch-dark, family members quickly remove the shoulder titles to expose the insignia of a second lieutenant. When the lights come back on, all the gentlemen cadets have magically turned into officers. My mother and I stood on either side of my brother, taking one epaulette each, and worked quickly to remove the shoulder titles. I remember feeling very nervous that I may fumble and not be fast enough for the job at hand before the lights came back on.

That reminds me of another story from that day: My brother wondered how he should address our father from then on, because not only was he his father, he was now also our brother's superior officer. So my brother started calling our father 'Daddy Sir' to cover both aspects. We all were very amused by this!

In the years that followed, with your brother being posted out to the remote corners of the country, did you get to see much of him?

Oh yes—we met often, although the visits were short. My brother was very good at staying in touch and visited me wherever I was. I eagerly anticipated these visits, which were fun and congenial. He always had interesting adventures to share. Sometimes we went to the movies. He loved movies about flying. One time, he wanted to watch *The Blue Max*, a movie about a German pilot, during WWI. I told him I didn't want to watch a movie with a German soldier as the protagonist. My brother replied that just because they were on the opposing side, didn't mean they weren't brave and talented. So off we went to the cinema, and I am glad we did, because it turned out to be an excellent movie. The flying sequences were breathtaking; I still remember the ecstatic look on his face when the pilot flew his plane under a bridge! To fly was what he wanted most in life.

Another one of his visits comes to mind: My husband was posted at Hindon and I had just been appointed as the secretary of the Air Force Wives Club. I had been asked to give my first speech, which was to introduce the newest venture of our club to help women earn an income by selling their handicrafts. I remember feeling extremely nervous, wondering what I was going to say. And then my brother—my white knight—came for a visit out of the blue. When I told him of my predicament, he asked me for a pen and a pad and locked himself in the guest room for an hour or less, and handed me a most beautifully written multi-page speech about female empowerment and tradecraft. There was one part I still remember clearly, where he called our club the 'Temple of Minerva'—Minerva being the Roman goddess of arts and trade. Needless to say, it was a big hit.

Even the commanding officer's wife pulled me aside later to tell me how moving my speech was. It was not the time to tell her then that the speech on women power was actually written by a man.

What year was that?

That was in 1970.

When we spoke earlier, we discussed your brother as he was in the early sixties and you painted a picture of a vigorous youth who was very much a part of the culture of that time. What about the late sixties? How did the events of that time affect your brother? I mean the rock-and-roll music and the free-your-mind hippie culture?

My brother of the late sixties was very different from my brother of the early sixties. Something happened to him in the intervening years. Sometimes I thought he had become a bit of a bore. Gone were the dancing and parties. Instead, he became monk-like. He had almost no personal possessions. His suitcase would have just a couple of sets of civvies (civilian clothing). He had one dark suit in case he found himself at a formal event, and lots of books. Lots and lots of books. Unfortunately for me, the person I was then, young and immature, I couldn't understand nor appreciate the beauty of this simplicity.

What sort of books? Do you recall what he was reading around that time?

I don't recall the names of the books, but the one common theme that ran through them was self-reliance and personal growth. I remember that he often quoted Ralph Waldo Emerson.[4] Emerson wrote this and Emerson wrote that, he would tell our mother. The first time I heard of Zen Buddhism was from him. He would talk about living simply and being self-reliant and resilient. Those were the genres of books he was reading at age twenty-one—the age when most young people are focused on having more and more in terms of material possessions, and here he was, far along on his journey to giving it all up.

I once asked him, 'Why have you created such a hard life for yourself? Don't you enjoy all the creature comforts as the rest of us do?' He replied, 'Yes, I do enjoy all this too. I get my fill of it when I visit you all.'

In hindsight, I can see the change in him was complete by the time he finished his training at NDA. His years there crystallized who he was becoming, slowly and gradually, since his late teens. And along with growing into a true embodiment of sheer goodness he was! I don't think anyone would dare to be less than their best selves in his presence—he inspired that in people … it is certainly true of me!

4

Soldiering
1968–1970

'Nothing can bring you peace but yourself.
Nothing can bring you peace but the triumph
of principles.'

—Emerson

1968

A train is snaking through the wilderness of southern Bihar (now called Jharkhand) with him peering out of one of its windows; he is taking in views of the countryside in which his parents have chosen to live out their retirement years.

When his parents had first written to him about finding their dream home in a place called McCluskieganj, he had been happy for them. But when his father had written that '. . . one day, you will be the inheritor of our estate', his mood had soured. Uncharacteristically, he had shot off a reply to his father saying their new house was for them, and not to count on him to establish himself there, as he knew with certainty how and where he wished to live his life. Furthermore, the thought of living a settled life in some city revolted him.

His harshly worded letter had not gone down well with his father. '*Daddy bahut naaraz huey teri chitthi padh kar,*' his mother had written to him, so he had quickly apologized for his words, although his thoughts on how to live his life hadn't changed.

The land he sees before him from the window of his train, however, piques his curiosity. It is unlike any he has seen before. Long stretches of forested hills extend as far as his eyes can see, occasionally broken by rivers swollen with monsoon rainwater. Rarely does he spot people, for the land is sparsely populated. It is the sort of place he could see himself living in.

Niki

[Author] *Mrs Kumar, a few years ago, when I was flying from Boston to San Francisco, I noticed that out of all the movies that were available on the airplane's entertainment centre, many of my co-passengers had chosen to watch* A Death in the Gunj.[1] *For a moment, I flirted with the idea of tapping each of them on the shoulder to tell them that the house in which the movie was filmed is the same house where Kamal would be living if he were still with us. I didn't have the courage to do it. Plus, then I would have had to explain who Kamal was and why he was no longer with us.*

Anyway, I wanted to ask you—how did that movie end up getting filmed in your house?

[N] The film director was scouting out houses in McCluskieganj, and she happened to choose mine.

I see. And how is it that the lead actor in the movie, Om Puri, ended up with your father's name 'Colonel O.P. Bakshi'?

My father's name plate is on the wall of the front veranda of the house. I guess the director decided to run with it.

Interesting indeed! And the house in McCluskieganj? I mean, how did your parents end up acquiring a house in such a remote place that few have heard of?

Around the time my father was approaching retirement from the Army, my parents started searching for a suitable home to live in. At one point, they looked at buying a plot of land in New Delhi, but they could not see themselves in a house hemmed in by neighbours in a crowded and noisy city. Then a friend of my father, Colonel Rana, told him about an idyllic little town called McCluskieganj. The town was, in fact, a commune started by a group of Anglo-Indians in the 1930s. After Independence, the commune had slowly started to break apart, with many of the original settlers heading off to the UK, Canada and Australia. That was when a few native Indians moved there and the trend continued. On visiting the commune, my parents had fallen in love with the house and had decided there and then that it would be the place they would call home after my father hung up his military boots.

It must have been a far cry from urban city life, living completely off the grid?

Yes, it was. They used coal braziers for cooking, kerosene lanterns for light, farmed their own vegetables and fruit and kept cows for milk. McCluskieganj did not offer the amenities of a city, so it attracted people of a certain bent— the type willing to put up with the hardships of country life in return for the bounty it offered. Even today, artists, philosophers and wanderers from all over the world find their way to McCluskieganj.

In a letter dated August 1968, your brother gave a brief report of his visit there. This is what he wrote: '. . . the place and our home are lovely and the people there very nice indeed . . . they are close-knit and know each other faithfully and well . . .' Is there anything else you recall your brother telling you about his impressions of McCluskieganj?

Nothing that I recall. But McCluskieganj is still like that; still the way my brother described it over fifty years ago.

Is that why you like to spend time in McCluskieganj?

Yes, it is my refuge. When life in London starts to feel hectic or gloomy during the wet winter months, I find myself longing for the simplicity and community of McCluskieganj.

Prithvi Jit

(Prithvi Jit Singh is a mechanical engineer and the founding member of the Indian Steam Railway Society. He is related to Kamal by marriage.)

[Author] *Mr Singh, how did you come to know Kamal?*

[P] I was distantly related to him through marriage. He looked me up when he got posted to Kota, the city I lived in back then. He told me he always sought family out wherever he went, no matter how distant the connection.

Do you have any recollections of meeting him all those years ago? Anything that he said that stands out in your mind?

I cannot remember anything specific that he said, but I recall enjoying our time together. He was an interesting chap—bright and earnest. That reminds me of something interesting about him. It just so happened that I was good friends with the commanding officer of his battalion, and it was from this CO that I heard this story: One day, the CO hauled Kamal into his office to reprimand him for some infraction. I do not remember what exactly Kamal had done, but it was something trivial. It was Kamal's first month in the Army and any young officer would have just faced the music and carried on with life. But not Kamal. He went to headquarters, found some book on Army regulations, and the next day politely explained to the CO that whatever he had done was, in fact, permissible within Army rules.

The CO must have been furious?

On the contrary, his CO found the whole affair very amusing. He had never met a second lieutenant like Kamal, who, despite having the lowest rank among officers then, had the courage to speak up when he felt he had been wronged.

Did Kamal ever talk about wanting to transfer to the Sikhs?

All the time. He kept petitioning the Army high command to transfer him to a Sikh regiment. He used to tell me time and time again that Sikhs were among the fiercest fighters in the world and that he wanted to fight alongside them. Hari Singh Nalwa[2] was someone he greatly admired; he knew all the obscure little details about Nalwa's many battles. It was all music to my ears, being a Sikh myself. Anyway, his perseverance paid off—he was reassigned to the Sikhs within a couple of months of our meeting.

July

It is the second to last day of a training course he is taking at The Infantry School in Mhow, Madhya Pradesh, and now he has some free time that he uses to write a letter to the younger of his two sisters. The two exchange letters regularly and now it is his turn:

Dear Nikiji,

A nice thunderstorm has developed outside, and the pleasant smell of rain fallen on dry ground is wafting in through the window. So must it be in Chandigarh, rain, and more rain.

Thank you very much for your letter and for the interesting description of your holiday. Bomdila (Arunachal Pradesh) and the surrounding countryside seem to be very pleasant and unusual to judge from what you have told me. And egged on by your account I shall certainly try and pay that area a visit.

I'm learning a thing or two about weapons here before going on to join my new unit (5 Sikh). You can write to me there in your own time as I shall take a couple of weeks off after this course finishes tomorrow. And do let me know whenever you feel a bit of finances would slightly improve life in general.

Your loving brother
Kamal

Lt. Colonel Kale

(Lt. Colonel Vishwas Kale is a retired Army officer. He was Kamal's senior and friend.)

[Author] *Colonel, when did you first meet Kamal?*

[CK] We met the day after he joined our battalion, 5 Sikh. I distinctly remember that it was evening time when he arrived because there was a formal get-together in the officers' mess.

Sorry to interject, but how does that work? I mean, what is the protocol for an officer joining a new battalion?

As per protocol, Kamal must have told the sentry at the gate that he was joining the battalion. The sentry would have informed the mess havildar, who in turn would have informed the battalion adjutant. Because Kamal was wearing civilian clothes, he could not join us in the mess, and so the adjutant directed him to his new quarters. The next morning, I went down to Kamal's quarters to formally welcome him into the battalion. Although he was junior to me, he made an immediate impression on me. He was different from other subalterns.

How so, sir?

Normally, a subaltern just tries to stay out of trouble and not draw too much attention to themselves as they are new to the battalion and at the bottom of the totem pole. But Kamal was never hesitant to put forward his views and opinions. He was also very articulate and passionate. It was evident from his eyes—the way they would sparkle when he spoke, and the crow's feet that would appear around them when he smiled.

Is there anything else you remember about him?

Oh yes! I remember him very well. His generosity and dependability come to mind. He did not earn much as a subaltern, yet he used to regularly send a money order to a nun who cared for him when he was a young boy in boarding school.

He was someone you could count on any time and every time. I remember one time I had invited my girlfriend to the officers' mess for dinner. Shortly after she arrived, the mess havildar informed me that the adjutant wanted to speak to me on the phone. The adjutant told me, 'Vishwas, I have detailed you for night firing.

The vehicle is waiting for you. See you at the firing range.' I put down the phone receiver and thought: *Oh hell! What do I do now?* Just then, I heard Kamal call out to me: 'Good evening, sir!' I told him of my predicament and asked him if he could entertain my dinner date in my absence. He agreed right away, as usual. Next day, my girlfriend rang up and kept praising Kamal: 'I had a wonderful time last evening with that captain. He is so nice, so interesting to talk to.' She also said that Kamal had given her a detailed tour of all the paintings in the officers' mess. She couldn't get over the fact that Kamal—who was just twenty-one at that time—knew all the obscure little details of the art and artists.

The fascinating thing about Kamal was that not only was he well-read and articulate, he was also very tough. It is rare to find a combination like that—someone who is bookish and brawny at the same time. He was fantastic at bayonet fighting; he could frighten off anyone who went up against him. He would also push himself physically to extremes. One time, I woke up at night to the sound of metal clinking in the open ground behind our barracks. It was Kamal, lifting weights at midnight! 'Just easing the body, sir,' he told me.

A very colourful chap all around—bright, curious, spirited, tough and always ready to have fun. We spent a lot of time together playing basketball, trekking and painting our barracks.

Were you with him during the war?

No, I was posted out of the battalion before the war. But I clearly remember the last time I met him. He was on parade duty on the morning I was leaving the battalion. He had asked the adjutant whether he could be excused from duty so as to see me off at the convoy ground, but the adjutant had refused him permission. Fortunately, there was a short pause in parade practice, so he sprinted the 4-kilometre distance between the parade and convoy grounds. He ran up to me just as I was climbing aboard my jeep and told me: 'Sir, you are one who knows me well. I will miss you.' Then he gave me a smart salute, turned on his heel and ran back to the parade ground. That moment is seared into my mind even though it occurred over fifty years ago. I feel very nostalgic whenever I recall it.

1969

Once again, he is packing his bags for his battalion has been handed its marching orders: this time they are to relieve the Maratha unit deployed alongside the border near a village called Chhamb. At the appointed hour, he makes his way to the head of the assembled men and leads them to their new destination.

∘∘∘

He was to be promoted to a lieutenant today, but there seems to have been a mistake. The bump up in his pay cheque is higher than he was expecting, and so he pays a visit to the adjutant's office where a pleasant surprise awaits him. It transpires that he has skipped a rank; instead of lieutenant, he has been promoted to captain. Unbeknown to him, the CO of his battalion had commended him for a double promotion based on his professional conduct and knowledge, which exceeded a person of his rank. He is pleased to learn that his CO holds him in high regard, for he feels the same way about his (then) CO.

∘∘∘

Because their new encampment lies within a few thousand yards of the border with Pakistan, and because war with their adversarial neighbour is always a possibility, he and his men live in a state of constant battle-readiness. Rigorous training, war games and nightly patrols are the norm for them. As for him, he has also set himself the personal goal of familiarizing himself with every nook and cranny of the territory that comes under his battalion's purview. And so, in his free time, he walks down every little track that criss-crosses the enclave to quickly familiarize himself with it. In a letter addressed to his younger sister, he gives a brief account of how he spends his days:

Dear Niki,

Thank you for your letters, all. I admit there has been a dearth of replies from me—but this in a month wherein I bathed only three times, and not because the cold said it. That means I was that busy.

Other things one could add as interesting topically: I brushed my teeth 7 times in that same space, ate a couple of weeks of hard rations, walked several hundred miles. I will tell you more when I meet you.

Yesterday the C.O. bid me proceed on annual leave and I'm going to Basar (Arunachal Pradesh) tomorrow. There I will stay for 15 days and then see the relative circle at Delhi for a week. Then I'll come and hob-nob with you for a bit.

Your news regarding Kiki (expecting) received with pleasure. I bet you D Day will be closer to my day than your day. Register this bet for a party at a good Chandigarh restaurant, Roger? Acknowledge this bet at Basar, Out!

Your loving brother,
Kamal

Niki

[Author] *Mrs Kumar, from your brother's letters, it seems he visited you often when you were in college. What were his visits like?*

[N] He would spoil me, like any big brother would, I suppose. He would take me out to nice restaurants and would tell me stories about his latest adventure.

What stories, if I may ask? Can you recall any?

There were so many. Let me think . . . One time, he visited me soon after completing a commando course in Mhow. He was a team leader, and his team came first but they were not awarded the Golden Dagger, the prize given to the top finisher. The reason was that after finishing first, my brother turned to the second-placed team leader, who happened to be senior in rank to him, and said, 'Sir, now you must surrender.' That did not go down well with the senior officer, who complained that my brother's words were not in the spirit of the games. So my brother's team was demoted.

Another time, he told me about his solo hike along the Teesta river near the Bengal-Sikkim border. One evening, after lighting a fire on the river's sand bank and settling into his sleeping bag, he spotted a tiger looking back at him. Even so, he stayed put and slept the night right there all alone. I asked him why he did that, and he said it was to overcome his fear. I told him it was a very dangerous thing to do, and he said he did have a *kukri* (knife) in case the tiger decided to pick a fight with him.

Then there was the time he walked from Chandigarh to Shimla. He was in Sanawar, walking past the Lawrence School, a boarding school, when it started to get dark. So, he asked the school gatekeeper if he could sleep in one corner of his cabin until dawn. The gatekeeper said he needed permission from school staff so off he went and returned with a teacher who told my brother that strangers were not allowed on school property. But then my brother and the teacher got talking and it turned out that before Sanawar, he used to teach in my brother's former school, Sherwood. The next thing my brother knew, he was being ushered into a guest house and getting fed a hot dinner!

He told me many stories like that: about the kindness of strangers and how they moved him. Another time, my brother was out walking in the hills and a poor old goatherd offered to share his meagre meal with him. That incident left a deep impression on him—he spoke about it often.

The kindness went both ways, for my brother was very generous too. Maybe too generous. I recall my mother complaining about him giving away his woollens to strangers in the winter. One time, he gave away his sleeping bag to a shivering passenger on a train.

Then there was this one time when he was heading home on leave, and decided on a whim that he would bicycle home instead of taking the train. He went to the Army canteen in Pathankot, bought himself a bicycle and rode it five hundred kilometres to New Delhi. When he reached our aunt's home, he gave his bike away to a poor man in the neighbourhood. He told our aunt that the bike had served the purpose it was bought for, and it was time to pass it on.

Undated photo of Kamal with the family dog.

June

His boarding school, Sherwood College, was established exactly a hundred years ago. To mark the centenary celebrations, the school has invited its former graduate, Lieutenant-General (later Field Marshal) Sam Manekshaw, as the chief guest.

To hear the popular general speak in person is one of the reasons he, Kamal, has come back to school. And when the time for the chief guest's speech rolls around, the general does not disappoint. From his very first sentence, he has the assembled crowd roaring with laughter.

'Your Grace, the Metropolitan of India, My Lord Bishop of Lucknow, Mr Principal, ladies, and young gentlemen of Sherwood: Yesterday evening, when my A.D.C. told me that I would have to speak here, I was horrified! I thought the principal had asked me to come and join the celebrations; I did not realize he wanted me to sing for my supper!'[3]

Shahid

[Author] *Dr Najeeb, in the photograph from your school's centenary celebration showing General Manekshaw surrounded by all the alumni, including you, I don't see Kamal. I know for a fact that Kamal attended that event. But then again, it is not surprising that Kamal is missing as he did not like being photographed. Do you know how he got out of that one?*

[S] Yes, Kamal is indeed missing from that photo. That is because he was playing the role of bodyguard when the photo was being taken.

Why would the general need a bodyguard?

Manekshaw was a big deal back then, not just in our school but in the entire country. After the Chinese war, Nehru had turned to Manekshaw to take charge of the eastern border. In fact, Manekshaw was headed to Delhi the day after our school centenary to be appointed Army Chief. So, Kamal was guarding the man he greatly admired.

*Did General Manekshaw know that Kamal was
watching his back while he was out rubbing elbows
with the masses?*

No. It was just something Kamal decided to do
on the spur of the moment. It was Kamal being
Kamal.

1970

November

He is walking past a row of houses in Hindon Air
Force Station, headed to the one where the elder of his
two sisters lives. Although he drops in often to meet
her, his visit today is to check in on her husband, who
is recovering from a recent flying accident.

Sumant

(Sumant Bakshi is a retired Air Force fighter pilot. He was Kamal's brother-in-law.)

[Author] *Sir, after your flying accident, one of the people to visit you in the hospital was your brother-in-law, Kamal. Do you recall his visit?*

[S] I do. He gifted me and Farokh—the other pilot—a bottle each of VAT 69 scotch. It is a very expensive whisky; must have cost him half a month's salary. He stayed with me for a while; he wanted to know everything that had happened.

What exactly happened, sir?

I was flying Hunters back then. Since I had not flown in a while, due to medical reasons, I was required to pass a check-out flight with a senior instructor, Squadron-Leader Farokh Mehta. On returning to base, Farokh told me to go around one more time. That meant taking off again, circling the airfield and landing. About a hundred feet in the air, the engine cut out and we started to lose altitude. I tried to relight the engine, but it wouldn't start. Then I tried to eject but the ejection seat canister did not fire. That is when I thought it was all over. But Farokh saved the day! If he had not shouted 'Alternate' at that very instant, I would not have pulled the backup ejection handle in time for both of us to get out.

As for Kamal, he was interested in my state of mind when all this happened. He wanted to know how one's mind behaves when faced with mortal danger.

What went through your mind, sir?

It froze. Then my wife and my daughter's faces flashed before my eyes. It happened in an instant.

How would you describe your relationship with Kamal? Were you two close?

I would not say we were close. There was a certain level of formality in his manner—not entirely surprising, because I think most Army officers tend to be a bit formal, as opposed to Air Force officers.

But even so, he was always considerate towards me. I will give you an example: Some years before my flying accident, I had developed stones in one of my kidneys. It happened when my squadron was posted in Assam, where some areas had drinking water that contained oil and sediments, and we had a very rudimentary water filtration system on the airbase. Drinking that water had caused me to develop those painful kidney stones, and my medical condition deteriorated to the point where my flying privileges were revoked. I met many doctors but my condition barely improved. Then one day, Kamal showed up and handed me a little packet. In fact, it was not even a packet but a small square of folded newspaper with some powder in it. He said he had got it from a highly recommended *hakeem* who lived in a little *gali* in Old Delhi. I was naturally concerned about ingesting some ash-coloured powder prescribed by a quack, but Kamal assured me it was safe. I asked him how he knew that, and he said he had been ingesting it for the past few days to test it on himself first. I was blown away when he said that.

Did it help with your condition?

Yes, it did. I started to take the powder as prescribed by Kamal and it made me urinate like crazy. Whatever was in my kidneys got flushed out and soon the pain disappeared. Now if you ask me: 'Was it that powder that cured me or was I on the mend anyway?' my answer is 'I don't know.' But I will never forget the fact that he took it upon himself to scour the country in search of a cure for my pain, and then tested it on himself before handing it to me. What a guy!

Going back to the time he came to meet you after the crash, was that the last time you met him?

Let me think . . . No, I met him again in the summer of 1971 when he came for my father's funeral. That reminds me of another incident involving him: The two of us were driving to Haridwar after the funeral to immerse my father's ashes in the Ganga, and my old uncle was with us in the car. This uncle was considered the authority on religion in our family and was explaining the spiritual concept of life and death to us when Kamal piped up and told us how he saw it. Now I do not remember what exactly Kamal said, but I do remember that he explained it very eloquently and respectfully. Even my authoritarian uncle, who had spent years studying the scriptures, fell silent after Kamal spoke and we drove in silence for a long time before anyone spoke. Kamal was twenty-four years old then, the same age as me. I remember thinking, 'Wow! This guy is the same age as me, and yet he speaks so clearly about such an obscure topic.' That was the last time I met him. The war broke out some months after that.

That summer of 1971, when you both took that road trip, did you both know that war was a certainty?

No. Not at that time. Conditions had been getting worse progressively, but it was only in the autumn of 1971 that one started to see large-scale military deployments along the border.

5

The Approaching Storm
1971

July 1971

In the *Illustrated Weekly of India*, a report on the deteriorating conditions on the eastern border:

Not Wanted in Pakistan
by
Khushwant Singh

General Jagjit Singh Aurora is the head of the Indian Army's Eastern Command. I asked him bluntly whether India will go to war against Pakistan.

'Not a fair question to ask a soldier,' he said, looking into his glass full of scotch. 'But you tell me what are we to do when five million refugees are forced on to us? We can't look after them and the world doesn't give a damn.'

---

ooo

He is inspecting the Border Security Force (BSF) outposts located alongside the border to familiarize himself with the terrain. If war breaks out, the BSF men will be ordered to pull back and his battalion will replace them. Their outposts, located within a few hundred yards of the border, provide an unobstructed view of the countryside and he can clearly see villagers going about their daily lives. The peaceful setting, however, belies the trouble brewing in the country across the border.

Pakistan is in turmoil because in the recently held elections—the very first general election to be held there since it became an independent country—the results had not favoured the West Pakistan-based political party preferred by the country's military establishment. Its military ruler had gone on to ignore the vote by not inviting the majority party from East Pakistan (now called Bangladesh) to form the next government, and as a result, the country had devolved into civil war. Thereon, instead of reflecting on his actions that had led to chaos in the first place, the military ruler had responded with an even heavier hand by sending in troops to brutally put down the insurgency in East Pakistan. Now, each day brings news of tens of thousands of refugees walking across the border from East Pakistan into India. There is also increased chatter about war, with India accusing Pakistan of pushing its unwanted Hindu citizens into India, and Pakistan accusing India of supporting its insurgents.

Because his battalion faces West Pakistan, he does not have to deal with the refugee crisis unfolding on the eastern border of the country, but the mood in his battalion has certainly shifted. He and his men have also stepped up reconnaissance patrols near the border while the senior commanders are reviewing their battle plans.

September 1971

The consensus reached by area commanders is that in the event of war, the best course of action for his battalion would be to break the advancing enemy's momentum in stages. Specifically, his unit is to resist the enemy around Chhamb for at least forty-eight hours to slow them down, before withdrawing 10 miles to a location tactically more advantageous to the Indians. Once there, they are to counter-attack the weary enemy and regain all lost territory.

Although the plan is controversial—it involves giving up their own territory before recapturing it—there is sound logic behind it: with the Kalidhar mountain range along their northern flank, the mighty river Chenab to their south, and the swiftly flowing Munawar Tawi river directly behind them, his battalion has little room to manoeuvre in Chhamb, and consequently has few options to outwit the enemy if attacked. Therefore, it is decided that to draw the enemy to a spot where the terrain favours the defenders would be better.

And so, with a tentative battle plan in place, he and his fellow men undertake rigorous drills to address all the possible scenarios that might result from it.

Colonel Handa

(Colonel Pradeep Kumar Handa is a retired Army officer. He was Kamal's batchmate in the National Defence Academy and his battalion's adjutant during the war.)

[Author] *Sir, you served in the same unit as Kamal. Were you friends?*

[CH] Yes, we were. I first met him in NDA where we both were cadets. We started out as batchmates, but then for some inexplicable reason he ended up graduating two batches after me. We reconnected when he joined my unit in Barrackpore.

What is the first thing that comes to your mind when you think back on him?

Someone tough as nails. Both physically and mentally. I recall one time walking past his room. It was a chilly winter morning and it felt even colder inside our cement-floored barracks. And there was Kamal—sitting on the cold floor, barechested and meditating. I was shocked and told him he would fall sick; he replied, 'Hands, don't worry, yaar. This is my daily morning regimen.' Hands was my nickname.

Another thing about Kamal was that he loved to read. I remember seeing him return to the battalion after his annual leave carrying a small backpack containing clothes and a large suitcase full of books.

As for his personality, he was a loner, kept mostly to himself. But he was not bashful when it came to speaking his mind, and that got him into trouble at times. He was what you would call a 'straight shooter'. He told you exactly what was on his mind; to him it did not matter if you were his contemporary or a general.

That reminds me of an incident: A sand model exercise[1] was to take place at the brigade headquarters and representatives from each of the infantry and artillery battalions had to attend. It just so happened that all the senior officers of our unit were either indisposed or on leave, so we ended up sending Kamal, who was just a captain, to an exercise with colonels and brigadiers. After the exercise was over, I got a call from headquarters asking, 'What is that thing you sent over?' I got worried, thinking, 'Oh no! What has Kamal done now?' But I was way off the mark. It turned out that Kamal had stood out for his excellent grasp of whatever was being discussed! At the end of the exercise, the colonel leading it turned to the brigadier (equal in rank to a one-star general), asking if he had any closing remarks. The brigadier replied: 'Gentlemen, I have nothing to add to what this captain has perfectly summed up.' That was a quite a remarkable thing for the brigadier to have said; a brigadier showing deference to a lowly captain in front of other officers is unusual. But then again, not a surprise in the case of Kamal, for that is the type of person he was—a gem of a guy who could hold his own against all.

October 1971

The rising probability of war has forced the generals to make a pre-emptive move—they have ordered his battalion to its battle stations, for they do not wish to be caught on the back foot if matters quickly take a turn for the worse. And so he is heading to a spot called Point 303[2] atop a ridge that offers commanding views of the land to the west, all the way up to the border; as per his battalion commander, he and his fellow mates of A Company are to dig in there with the objective of fending off any enemy infiltration past it.

o o o

Of the more than 120 men who make up A Company, he ranks second in the chain of command. His superior officer is a major with whom he confers daily to plan and implement defences in their theatre of operation. The area they have been tasked with defending—a 2000-yard-wide by 3000-yard-deep swath of land between the border and the ridge—encompasses three villages, a causeway linking the three, farmland and a dry riverbed. To defend it all, they have at their disposal four rifle platoons of thirty men each, two medium machine guns (MMGs) and three recoilless rifles (RCLs) capable of knocking out tanks. For all the challenges they must anticipate and plan for, perhaps the most pressing one for him is to convince the villagers to clear out and move inland, with the oldest villagers proving to be the most obstinate:

'Please leave now before it is too late,' he implores them.

'What about our livestock? Who will feed them? They are all we have,' they retort.

November 1971

The big boss, Army Chief Sam Manekshaw, has helicoptered in for a first-hand inspection of war preparations in Chhamb. When briefed of the defensive battle plan, however, the chief makes it clear that he is not on board. The thought of ceding even a single yard of own territory to the enemy is unacceptable to him, leave alone 10 miles of it. What he wants, instead, is for the forces in Chhamb to go on the offensive, to protect own territory by capturing the opponent's.

The new orders mean that his battalion's role has now changed: no longer are they to act as the advance guard that fights a retreating battle; instead, they are to stay put and defend Chhamb until the very end.

∘ ∘ ∘

He is writing a letter home. It will be the second to last letter his parents will get from him.

My dear Mummy and Daddy,

I am well and happy, in fact in peak form. I hope all is similarly well in Kumarsain.

I am leading the life of a country squire here. Morning P.T. in bracing weather starts the day auspiciously, followed by breakfast wherein are served the countryside's products. The area is thick with partridge and I go out often on a borrowed gun. Then preparation and polish up on the task at hand.

I am reading *Cassino: Portrait of a Battle* in spare times and have arrived at the 'Second Battle' where the Indians and New Zealanders take over from the US 5th Army and the Royal Sussex of 7 Brigade. Mention is also made of the 4/16th Punjabis and the 4/6th Rajputana Rifles. I have yet to read about 5 Brigade and the other remaining one. I wonder which was yours Daddy, I would like to read about it in the book.

Now I close.

Your loving son,
Kamal

Atul

(Atul Bakshi is a glass artist whose works can be found in homes and corporate offices across the world. He was Kamal's brother-in-law.)

[Author] *Sir, you were the last family member to meet Kamal right before the war. How did that come about?*

[A] He had been granted a short leave, so he hopped on to a military truck to come to Amritsar to meet his sister, who was married to my older brother. But no one was home except for me, so he ended up spending those two days with me.

Do you remember anything from those two days?

I remember everything. I remember those two days vividly. I was fourteen years old back then, and he was the person I looked up to the most. I still feel fortunate to have got to spend those two days with him.

There is one incident I can never forget because it made a deep impression on me. On his way down to Amritsar, he had stopped at Pathankot where a medical doctor friend of his was posted. His friend needed a new stethoscope. So, in the morning, when I was heading to my school, he borrowed my bicycle and rode over to the medical supply store to buy the stethoscope, then rode 80 kilometres to Pathankot to deliver it, and then another 80 kilometres back to Amritsar, that same day! All that effort to help out a friend! That was the sort of man he was.

Anything you said to him received his full attention. If you told him that something was troubling you, he would dive deep into finding a way out of your quandary. Or, if you told him that you wanted to have fun, he would jump on his feet and say, 'Let's go! Let's have some fun!'

One night, just before going to bed, I told him that I wanted to be tough and fit like him. Next morning, at the crack of dawn, he woke me up saying, 'You said you wanted to get fit. Let's start now.' So off we went running down Mall Road. I remember many jawans stopped to salute him, recognizing him as an officer because of his white clothes and short hair, but he would not return their salute; instead, he acknowledged them by straightening his arms and stiffening his back. I remember asking him why he did not return their salute and he told me that you only return a salute when you are in uniform.

In the evenings, he would play his bagpipes for me. He would play marching tunes in our courtyard, and I would march behind him.

He also told me he wanted to play his pipes atop a 10,000-foot-high mountain someday. Why 10,000 feet, you ask? Because it is very hard playing pipes in thin mountain air. That was the sort of man he was—always setting himself goals and reaching beyond them.

There was one other incident I recall. He told me he needed to buy underwear, so I took him to a shop in Hall Bazar where he specifically asked the shopkeeper for Jockey undies. How is it that I remember the brand name of the underwear after fifty years? Like I said, I hero-worshipped the man; everything one's hero says, one remembers. In fact, he bought me a pair too. He said they were the most comfortable undies and that a man must be comfortable when girding his loins for battle.

Our last moment together was early in the morning when I awoke and walked over to his room to say goodbye. I found him sitting on the side of his bed with a smile on his face and polishing his boots. Then he slipped on his boots, strapped on his backpack, hugged me and left.

Even though I never saw him again, he influenced the ways I chose to live my life. In fact, I can honestly say that no one has ever influenced me as much as he did with his integrity, his generosity and his strength.

29 November 1971

He is in his quarters reading, as he often does when he has some free time. The book he is reading presently is a retelling of the WWII battle fought around an Italian town called Cassino, in which over 55,000 Allied troops suffered casualties over a period of four months while attempting to uproot the well-entrenched Germans. One of those casualties had been his father—enemy gunfire had injured him in a leg and a hand, and he had spent the rest of the war in an infirmary in Italy. In fact, he has just received a letter from his father describing what being in battle is like. As per his father, it is like taking a cold-water shower—after the initial shock, the body grows numb to what follows.

Later, he pens another letter to his parents. It will be the last letter his parents get from him.

> My dear Mummy and Daddy,
>
> Thank you very much for your letter. Since last writing things are fairly quiet here.
>
> I faithfully touched my head on reading of your Kaziranga trek. It was terrific sir, though not surprising, since I've long known my O.C. to be the best ever and his unit (our family) truly the best possible.
>
> General Rommel did receive, because of the common German's esteem for him, a state funeral and burial whereat Von Rundstedt delivered a eulogy.

Otherwise, Hitler feared, any attempt to discredit the great general would be ill-tolerated.

Thank you for your apt description of battle experience—a cold water shower—it was very understandable, and I know now how to expect reacting to any future infantry involvement.

Yesterday the eye and hand were keen and in two very sportive shots I downed two partridge—my first flying. Both flew from right to left; I followed Michael Brander's instructions in *The Game Shot's Vade Mecum* each time correctly mounting the gun—a J. Stevens single barrel hammer—swing along with & through and the No 6 Sellier Bellot shot patterned true.

Game shooting, in addition, appears an effective method of acquainting oneself with the terrain militarily as one remembers the topography circumstant to the incidents in the shoot.

I did stay two days in Amritsar. Only Atul and his grandfather were present and of these, Atul had school between 8 and 2. I covered more reading and made a couple of purchases for field conditions in Atul's absence.

Now I close.

Your loving son,
Kamal

30 November 1971

A dispatch rider from headquarters has brought along printed forms for designating a beneficiary to one's estate in case of death. Because filling them out is mandatory, he does, but it is a pointless exercise for he possesses almost nothing; certainly nothing that holds much monetary value. His worldly possessions include a set of bagpipes, a sleeping bag, his newest acquisition—he gave away his last one to a shivering co-passenger on a train ride he recently took—and a handful of books that he is yet to read. After scanning through the form, he designates his mother the beneficiary of his few worldly possessions and his life insurance. His signature must also be attested by two witnesses and for that he turns to the major and the second lieutenant, who readily oblige.

2 December 1971

It is early morning and he is being briefed by the major on the latest orders from headquarters calling off the strike that had been in the works for the past month; instead of the attacking formation that the brigade had taken up almost a month ago, all battalions are to fall into a defensive posture within forty-eight hours. The new orders do not affect the platoons deployed around Point 303, for their task has always been the defence of the ridgeline, but it does affect their lone platoon of thirty men positioned 3 km ahead near Moel village, just a few hundred yards shy of the border. Up until now, the platoon near Moel had the responsibility of supporting the Indian strike column when it broke out. Now, with its mission limited purely to a defensive one, that platoon must seal off all the pathways purposely left open to provide passage to Indian troop movement. And since it is fair to assume that they are being watched incessantly by enemy scouts, all work of repositioning men, and laying anti-tank mines, must be done discreetly, under cover of darkness.

6

The Longest Hours
3–6 December 1971

[Author's Note: Since Kamal did not leave any note or letter describing his three days in the battle of Chhamb, the author has taken the liberty of recreating the battle based upon first-hand accounts of men who were present with him, and information gathered from several books and news articles about the battle written by Indian and Pakistani Army officers.]

3 December 1971

Morning

He is holding down the fort at Point 303, for the major has gone over to Moel village to take stock of matters there. The major had departed soon after headquarters sent word that the strike has been called off and therefore all gaps in defences, intentionally created to let their own tanks pass through, had to be sealed off immediately.

Being the seniormost officer while the major is away, it now falls on him to oversee the hundred-odd men there and to attend to dispatch riders bringing in the latest orders and the vehicles ferrying in supplies.

Afternoon

He has visitors: a colonel (his CO) and a brigadier (his CO's superior) have come up to inspect his post first-hand. After inspecting the placement of his platoons, their lines of fire, siting of the mortars and other miscellanea, the brigadier wishes him luck and moves on to the next post located some 3000 yards to his north.

6 p.m. (approximately)

An uneasy calm has descended over his post atop the ridge for he has just received a red alert over the wireless. As per the alert, Pakistani fighter jets have simultaneously bombed several airfields across the country, and so the war is officially on.

Exactly what comes next is anyone's guess. As per the most recent intelligence reports, the enemy strength directly across the border is one infantry brigade at the most,[1] making the two adversaries evenly matched in numbers. But the bigger unknown is whether the Pakistanis intend to fight along the Western Front at all, or whether they will limit their efforts to the Eastern Front since that is the entire basis of this war.

In the meantime, while they wait for the Pakistanis to reveal their hand, all he and his compatriots can do is to watch the border vigilantly while the twittering of birds settling in for the night fills the air around them. Occasionally, though, the chirping sound is punctuated by the crackle of the wireless set as it comes alive with the latest report.

9.30 p.m.

Sandbags are all that separate him and his men from certain death for the skies are raining destruction down all around them. Exactly 40 minutes earlier, Pakistani artillery guns had started to let loose along the entire perimeter of the Chhamb sector, plastering Indian defences with round after artillery round, without pause. The fact that his post is getting attended to by the Pakistanis does not surprise him, for they are well aware of its strategic importance, considering that Pakistani forces had occupied it briefly in 1947 and in 1965, and therefore know the area well. But what does surprise him is the intensity of bombardment raining down not just on him but over the entire sector.[2] With wireless reports streaming in of the enemy targeting the entire sector concurrently for such a long duration of time, he can tell that the enemy has brought along a serious amount of firepower[3] to the fight and therefore must have a larger design in mind than what Indian intelligence services had been led to believe.

Sometime before midnight

The opening barrage of Pakistani guns has died down. Now, artillery shells land on his post, not continuously but intermittently and unexpectedly, no doubt to harass his men and keep them pinned down in their foxholes. In the relative safety of the reduced shelling (but heightened danger, for the artillery shells now strike unpredictably), he heads out to take stock of matters, but visibility is poor; a thick cloud of dust and smoke envelopes Point 303. However, he is pleased to learn that his defences are largely intact. Most of his men are in high spirits but a handful are shaken, which is to be expected, for no amount of training prepares one for hours of artillery shells blasting a few yards away with only some sandbags providing protection.

Sometime past midnight

Two thousand yards to his north, at the other end of the ridge, is positioned D Company, and he can tell that it is under attack: he can see machine gun tracer shots streaking through the night sky towards it and he can also see its fiery ripostes. Over the wireless, he can also listen in on the running commentary between the D Company commander and headquarters.

He is surprised to see D Company get drawn into a firefight so early in battle for it can only mean one thing: that D Company's forward observation post along the border (that took many months of planning and preparation to set up) must have fallen.

Shortly thereafter, headquarters confirms his thoughts: that the observation post at Pir Jamal had indeed been steamrolled by an overwhelmingly large number of enemy tanks and infantry right after the shelling had eased, giving the enemy a free run to the ridge.

But not all the news is gloomy: incredibly, his own company's observation post at Moel is still intact! Somehow, the platoon there withstood the lethal artillery onslaught and the ferocious tank charge that followed it. He does not know how the men there pulled it off, but he suspects the major's presence there must have played a role in it.

In any case, the implications of events so far, the good and the bad, are clear to him—it means that all

Indian territory to his north-west is now under enemy control and it is only a matter of time before he can expect trouble from that direction. And sure enough, after the attack on D Company dies down (save for the artillery shells that continue to rain down on them and on him), it is his post that comes under attack. It starts with the dull thudding sound of machine gun fire hitting sandbags around his command post. Right away, his MMG detachments respond with a long volley of fire in the direction of the incoming fire. The firefight does not last long and is soon over. Once more, he heads over to check on the men and finds them positively amped up.

'We sent them packing; they ran away,' the men report.

'Well done!' he tells them. 'But stay sharp. It is possible they were just probing our defences before plotting their next move.'

4 December 1971

Daybreak

After a night of alarming reports, he is finally met with a welcome sight—the major has returned. After walking in the dark across minefields, artillery bombardment, small arms fire from both sides and evading enemy scouts, the major has miraculously returned and now he is being welcomed back with open arms by all.

When the short celebration finally breaks up, he briefs the major on the night's developments—the fall of the border posts to the north, and of the short skirmish with an enemy advance party late in the night. The major, in turn, gives him news of Moel: the platoon there had come under withering artillery fire but the men had held on stoutly, although some of the younger recruits had been a little shaken by the opening barrage. In fact, the major had wanted to stay on with the platoon there, but headquarters had turned down his request, instead ordering him to return to the ridge where the next phase of the battle was expected to play out.

Morning

His eyes are fixated on the tank-on-tank battle unfolding ahead of the ridge. The battle had started earlier in the morning, when the Assam Regiment men to his immediate south, near the village of Barsala, had come under attack. Being from a different battalion, his wireless is not tuned in to theirs, but the unfolding fight is visible from his post. Dust clouds had shrouded Barsala when enemy tank shells struck it, but the Assamese had put up a stiff resistance and thwarted the Pakistani advance. Unable to make headway, the enemy tanks had changed tack and manoeuvred north towards the base of the ridge, but there they had been challenged by a troop of Indian tanks. Now, as he keeps a close eye on the tanks from the two sides slugging it out, he stands ready to respond if the enemy tanks prevail and make a move towards the ridge.

Afternoon

Of the four companies that make up his battalion, three are in the throes of battling men and tanks, with his being the odd one out. Two thousand yards to his north, the men of D Company are facing off against a squadron of Pakistani Sherman tanks. Another 2000 yards to their north-west, near village Gurha, C Company is getting hammered by an even larger Pakistani force. And further west, up on the Mandiala Heights, B Company is getting a pasting from a yet larger enemy contingent.

The reason the enemy have been unable to attack A Company (his company) in strength is because of the intrepid platoon in Moel. Incredibly, even after 15 hours of battle, the courageous men in Moel are continuing to wreak havoc on Pakistani attempts to advance along the causeway leading to Point 303. If the Pakistanis attempt to drive along the causeway, the platoon thwarts their progress with small arms fire; if Pakistani supply trucks appear anywhere in the vicinity of Moel, the platoon calls in artillery strikes[4] to halt their progress.

Colonel Brar

(Colonel Gurcharn Singh Brar is a retired Army officer. He was Kamal's senior.)

[Author] *Colonel, thank you once again for agreeing to meet me.*

[CB] You said you are related to Kamal. How exactly?

I am his nephew.

I see. And how did you find me?

Your name is mentioned in General Khanna's book. An acquaintance helped me find your phone number.

I see. Well, it is nice to meet you. What can I do for you?

I was hoping you could tell me a little about Kamal as he was in the same battalion as you. Did you know him well?

I did know him. I wouldn't say I knew him well as he was much junior to me. I was already a company commander when Kamal joined our unit as a fresh recruit.

Was he assigned to your company?

No. He reported to Major Devinderjit Pannu, the A Company Commander. I was commanding C Company, so our interaction was less. But we did socialize. He was an interesting chap. Very well-informed. An engaging talker.

Could we talk a little about the war, sir? I read in General Khanna's book that C Company was positioned near Gurha.

That is correct. There was a little dirt track that ran past Gurha on the way to the battalion and brigade headquarters. My job was to make sure the enemy did not get past it.

I read that Gurha saw a lot of action. Several Pakistani accounts of the battle also mentioned Gurha by name.

Is that right? Well, I can tell you for a fact that it was four days of intense fighting. The enemy came in strength. A regiment worth of tanks. There was a nullah ahead of my post and the Pakistanis chose to launch their attack along it. At one point, I could see all their armour strung out in front of my post. All those tanks would have made a plum target for our Air Force jets if they had only shown up. The Indian Air Force could have wiped all of them out in one stroke, but they never came.

I read somewhere that the Indian Air Force was active in Chhamb . . .

Yes, they were. But that was after we were ordered to pull back behind the river. The river clearly demarcated the line between us and the enemy, making it a little easier for the pilots to target Pakistani armour.

Anyway, we did our best at holding back the enemy during the first four days of the battle. At one point, they managed to capture my post, but my men and I counter-attacked and knocked them back.

I believe you were wounded? General Khanna's book mentioned it.

Yes, I was. When I was attacking the enemy, my Sten carbine got jammed. Those guns could be unreliable at times. While I was sorting mine out, I got hit by a burst from an enemy carbine. Luckily, my wounds were not fatal. After six surgeries and a year in various hospitals, I was back in business.

While you were fighting your fight, were you aware of what was going on at the other company posts? Specifically at Point 303, where Kamal was?

I had an idea. We were all on the same wireless frequency so I could listen in to what was going on with the neighbouring companies. We were all in a similar position, all were fighting a ping-pong style battle: the enemy would come up to capture our posts and we would knock them back, over and over again.

As for Point 303, I spoke with the men there after the war was over. They had a tough fight on their hands as well. No one knew what happened to Kamal.

Did they mention anything about him in the lead-up to the day he went missing?

Well, now that you have asked, I will be frank. Maybe Kamal was a little too brazen in battle. I heard that he took unnecessary risks by going right up to the enemy's positions to keep an eye on them, closer than he needed to get. That might not have been the wisest thing for him to do.

Maybe he had good reasons for doing what he did.

Maybe so.

Evening

His radio operator is unable to hail the platoon in Moel and the implications of that are obvious to him—the platoon must have fallen.

It is disheartening news, for the men there had fought well indeed—even though they had been cut off from their own side, they had continued to fight for two days and had surely sown chaos in the enemy's plans.

The loss of Moel also means the enemy can now get a free run down the causeway leading all the way to the base of the ridge. It is only a matter of time before the enemy will be appearing at his doorstep.

Darshan Singh

(Sepoy Darshan Singh is a retired Army soldier. He reported to Kamal during the war.)

[Author] *Darshan Singh ji, you said you were taken POW during that war. How did that come about?*

[DS] I was the signals specialist attached to the platoon in Moel. My job was to maintain communications between the troops and headquarters. After fighting for two days, we ran out of ammunition and were overpowered by the enemy.

Your men did fight very bravely in Moel. The Pakistanis also acknowledged how brave your platoon was to keep fighting for two days, even when your post was surrounded.[5] I wanted to ask you, what happened at Moel once your ammunition ran out?

After our ammunition ran out, there was nothing we could do, and the enemy started closing in on us. They did not notice me in the tall *sarkanda* (grass), so I stayed put until it got dark and then started to walk back towards Point 303. Unfortunately, an enemy patrol noticed me and took me prisoner. Eventually, I was transferred

to the POW camp in Lyallpur where I remained
for a year before being repatriated to India.

Late evening

The firefight ahead of the ridge has finally broken out
and he is in it. His primary concern is to make sure the
men train their fire where it is needed most, and not
fire indiscriminately. 'Aim before you fire, and make
each shot count' is what he has told the men many
times before and does so again.

Night

With the enemy assembling in ever-larger numbers
ahead of the ridge, and the obvious conclusion that
they are readying for an assault on Point 303, he has
been ordered to pull his men back to the ridgeline to
reinforce it.

Late night

He is moving from bunker to bunker, checking on
the men, attending to those in need, offering words
of encouragement for the battle ahead. He also brings
news that is sure to cheer them up: in anticipation of
the attack they are about to face, headquarters has
dispatched three tanks to reinforce their position.

But there is also some unpleasant news from headquarters that he would rather not share with the men. Although C and D Companies had successfully thwarted the enemy's advance earlier in the day, that had not been the case with B Company. The enemy had sent a column of tanks down a narrow dry riverbed—a move that Indian commanders had not anticipated—and in the ensuing battle, the strategically located northern peak at Mandiala had fallen into enemy hands. The loss of the peak would not have been cause for too much alarm were it not for the fact that it offered a direct view of the bridge over the river and of Indian troop movement further inland. The enemy now had the potential to make matters very difficult for all of them.

5 December 1971

Daybreak

It is the hour before sunrise and he and his fellow men are standing to, with weapons drawn and at the ready in case the enemy springs a surprise attack. He knows that early mornings can be the most dangerous time for a defender—it has been so since the invention of warfare—as they are unable to see all the preparations an attacker has been making in the dark of the night. And so, expecting the worst while hoping for the best, he, and all his fellow company men—including the ones whose turn it is to snatch a power nap—are wide awake, alert and at the ready for whatever may come their way.

However, when the darkness finally lifts and he peers out, a peculiar scene unfolds in front of his eyes. He sees a column of enemy tanks blasting away at enemy infantrymen, and the infantrymen firing back at the tanks. After a moment of bafflement, he guesses what is going on—the two warring parties have mistaken each other to be Indians. To his disappointment, they eventually realize their mistake, settle their differences with verbal insults and turn their collective wrath towards the ridge. But his men are ready and respond equally forcefully.

Late morning

The early morning firefight has petered out without a clear winner. The Pakistanis had been unable to punch their way through his company's defences, while his company, in turn, had been unable to land a punishing enough blow to send the enemy packing. Now, the enemy has returned to slinging artillery and mortar at his post. In the intermittent pauses, he heads out once more to take stock of matters and finds that his defences are intact. So are the men's spirits, but there are some wounded who need attending to. The biggest loss of the skirmish has been a tank—it had taken a direct hit and is now out of commission.[6]

Noon (approximately)

There is a let-up in shelling and the reason for it soon becomes clear to him: enemy fighter jets, which have been hounding his battalion since the previous morning, are back. F-86 Sabres in particular have been a nuisance to his men through the daylight hours, strafing them or rocketing them or both.[7] This time, however, their prey is someone other than him or the tanks supporting his company. Instead, the enemy jets seem focused on something further behind him. He sees wave upon wave of Sabres pass directly overhead before they unload their munitions on a spot to the north-east of him. Exactly what they are gunning for he does not know, but what he does know is that there are several Indian assets of high value in that direction, including the bridge and the artillery batteries that support him.[8]

Afternoon

The last wave of Sabres has passed and artillery bombardment on his position has resumed with renewed vigour. The bombardment forces his men to seek shelter and the cloud of dust that envelopes them reduces their visibility down to nothing. He knows that moments such as these are often the prelude to a surprise attack and so he tells his men to remain on the alert.

Late afternoon

A most unfortunate event has just occurred: an artillery shell has landed just a few yards away from the major and now he is gravely wounded. 'Don't worry about me. I still have my left arm. I can still fire a weapon,' the tough-as-nails major says,[9] moments before losing consciousness.

After radioing the news to headquarters and helping the wounded major on to the jeep that is to take him to the infirmary, he informs the men about the major's mortal wounds. And as he speaks, his temper begins to rise. And for the first time ever, he lays bare his emotions in front of his men.

The men, in turn, are startled to hear him—the officer who rarely speaks unless spoken to and whom they privately refer to as the 'quiet one'—yelling at the top of his lungs: 'We will take revenge for what they did to the major—won't we? WON'T WE?'

He does not have to wait long for the revenge he seeks. Soon after, his post is showered with gunfire as an entire enemy battalion, backed by tanks, makes its way up the ridge. It is the moment he has been waiting for. The moment all his men have been waiting for. To finally take matters into their own hands. No more being shot at by unseen men firing from guns hidden miles away, or from jets that come roaring overhead and leave before you know it. Now it is man to man.

And it is personal. The enemy hurt their beloved major and now they will make them pay for it.

With a roar, he yells out the Sikh call to arms and his men respond with fervour and tear into the onrushing enemy. Hand-to-hand fighting ensues as the leading enemy troops reach the top of the ridge, but he and his men refuse to yield; each fighting with a fury that no enemy would want to face. Again and again, the enemy come up the ridge in waves, and each time he and his men push them back. It is after sundown when the enemy make one last attempt at wresting away his post, and then too, they are beaten back by him and his men.[10]

8 p.m. (approximately)

He is congratulating the men, for their efforts have indeed been extraordinary: even though their numbers were down to only two platoons, so determined had been their stand, and so courageous their counter-attacks, and so ferocious their hand-to-hand combat, they had managed to repel[11] an entire battalion of attackers. It was an impressive feat, and he tells them so.

The latest fight has also been a revelation for him. Although he had never doubted their courage, there had been times in the lead-up to the war when he wondered how his team would fare when they truly had their backs against the wall—would they hold the line with the valour that Sikh fighters are renowned for? Or would they scatter under pressure? But now, after having seen his men in their element, he doesn't harbour any doubts of what they are capable of. Instead, he is filled with admiration. His only regret is that the major—the only other person in this world who would have shared his sentiments—is no more. Headquarters had radioed him informing him about the major's passing. If he could, he would go to the ends of the earth to tell the major what had gone down at the ridge that evening. He is sure the major's chest would have swelled with pride, just as his has.

Late night

He has a new enemy to face—fatigue. Although his men are rightly chuffed from their recent win, he knows they are weary. The fight to which they gave their all has taken a physical toll on them, and the fact that none of them have had restful sleep in over 60 hours has left them all worn out.

He is weary too—being hypervigilant and sleep-deprived for over two days takes a toll on the best of men, and he is no exception—but loath to admit it and does his best not to let on. He cannot let his fatigue show for the men have put their trust in him— their full faith that he, their officiating company commander, will remain alert and level-headed to see them through whatever it is that the enemy unleashes on them.

But even though he remains steady and exudes confidence, there are matters that trouble him. Foremost on his mind is the fact that the latest victory came at a steep price—he lost far too many men. At the start of the war, his company comprised four platoons; now only two platoons worth of men remain. If the enemy attempted a repeat attack, his remaining men would have to shoulder a greater burden than they had to earlier in the day.

It also frustrates him to think that while he ponders how to further stretch his already stretched platoons, barely 500 yards away in village Upparli Banian, the enemy is likely regrouping and rearming themselves for another go at the ridge. What he would love to do at that point is to lead a swift and lethal raid on the enemy to disrupt whatever it is they are hatching. But his orders are to stay put, to hold fast the ridge and not let the enemy through.

Nachhattar Singh

(Sepoy Nachhattar Singh is a retired Army soldier and a politician in Punjab. He reported to Kamal during the war.)

[Author] *Nachhattar Singh ji, you saw Kamal on the night of 5 December. Can you recall that meeting?*

[NS] On 5 December, my duty was to guard the Battalion HQ in Sakrana. But then I was assigned a new task—I, along with five others, were ordered to head over to Point 303 as they needed reinforcements. There I reported to Captain Bakshi, and he assigned us to the platoons. It was just a short interaction.

Did you know him before that?

Oh yes! I used to meet him just about every day. Starting from early morning PT and during the afternoon sports hour, he would be there with us. I still remember all those cross-country runs we ran, with him in the lead pulling us along. I remember trying to get him to go easy on us. I would tell him: so-and-so's wife just gave birth, so why don't we celebrate by sleeping in tomorrow morning and skipping the run? He would always hear me out patiently and sometimes he would give in, but not always. He was a good officer. I liked him.

6 December 1971

Some hours before dawn

His command post is located between his two platoons, allowing him to keep an eye on both. With him in the post are two others: Sepoy Mohan Singh, whose responsibilities include manning the portable but bulky radio set and always staying within sight of him in case he needs to communicate with headquarters urgently, and Havildar Ajit Singh, whose responsibilities include assisting him in all matters, including relaying messages to his platoon leaders.

It is some hours before daybreak when the shelling on his post pauses and only gunfire and mortar can be heard. He and the men brace for an enemy onrush, but none occurs. Instead, enemy gunfire dies as abruptly as it had begun, and artillery shells start to rain down on his post.

It is the second time that night that the enemy has feigned an attack; the first one had occurred an hour or two after midnight. And although he understands what the enemy is getting at—harassing him and his men with fake punches to tire them out—there is little he can do besides treating each attack as if it is the real one.

6 a.m. (approximately)

His post is being showered with gunfire once more and this time the firing does not let up, with arms of every calibre joining in the chorus: the whizz of rifle shots, the higher-pitched staccato of light machine guns, the deeper-toned medium machine guns. One of his platoon leaders confirms what he already suspects—several hundred enemy troops are coming up the ridge. Shortly thereafter, the second platoon leader reports a similar number headed his way as well. All in all, a battalion worth of enemy troops, he reckons—about the same number his men faced the prior evening—before radioing headquarters about the rematch that is about to unfold at his post.

If the numbers of the enemy swarming the ridge alarm him, he does not belie his concern in front of the men, telling them that he has full confidence in their abilities and that victory will be theirs if they fight with the same vigour as they had the night before. But even so, though he knows there is no shortage of courage in his ranks, he knows the numbers do not favour his men. His platoons are outgunned eight to one, a difference too large for his men to handle unless they get some help to relieve the pressure on them. And so he radios headquarters and asks for artillery fire to be brought down on the enemy immediately; he needs it to thin out their advancing columns to more manageable numbers.

Meanwhile, while he waits for his request to be passed along the chain of command to those who will decide how much priority it deserves, he orders his mortar men to continue to fire the handful of light mortars available to them as furiously as they can.

6.30 a.m. (approximately)

The artillery support he had requested has not materialized yet. And if his need for it had been acute up to this point, now it is past critical, for a new and much more dangerous threat has just emerged before his eyes. In the gradually improving visibility of the early morning light, he sees a procession of enemy Sherman tanks gloriously stretched out along the causeway and heading directly towards his post. There are over a dozen of them and soon, they begin blasting their cannons at his men.

Hakam Singh

(Subedar Hakam Singh is a retired Army soldier. He reported to Kamal during the war.)

[Author] *Hakam Singh ji, you were up on Point 303 on the morning of 6 December. Can you please describe your recollections?*

[HS] We faced a massive attack on the morning of 6 December from enemy troops. And then enemy tanks also showed up. Many, many tanks. We were completely outgunned. I ran to the lone tank supporting us at Point 303 and I implored the crew to return fire. They told me there was nothing they could do as the tank was disabled. But I could hear the engine running so I called them out on that. 'How is it that the tank engine is still running if the tank is disabled?' I asked. They told me they were only running the engine to recharge the radio batteries, that the tank itself could not be manoeuvred. Then it was just us men against all those enemy tanks. We fought as best as we could.

What was it like up on the ridge that morning? I mean . . . what is it like to be in war?

War is chaotic. There is gunfire and shelling and dust getting kicked up and blood being spilt.

> The tall sarkanda around us was ablaze, so there was also a lot of smoke. That is what war is like.

6.45 a.m. (approximately)

Once again, he radios headquarters requesting artillery support—he needs it without a moment to spare, and he needs not just a single battery but each and every battery in the division to pummel the enemy tanks and infantrymen across the entire flank of his post. If the guns engage immediately, it might, just might, give his men enough of a break to turn the tide of the battle they are engaged in, he tells headquarters.

But the reply he gets from headquarters is stunning—there is no artillery support available, not a single battery; all the guns are in the process of pulling back behind the river because the Indian commanders are concerned about them falling into enemy hands.[12] As for the large-calibre long-range guns that were positioned in Kacheral, behind the river, they too are unavailable as they had been destroyed the previous day by enemy fighter jets. And so he will have to make do without any artillery support, comes the reply from headquarters.

Colonel Rasam Katoch

[Author] *Colonel, let us imagine the following scenario: an infantry company comprising two platoons is under direct attack by an enemy battalion (over twelve platoons) and a squadron of tanks (approximately fifteen tanks). Since you yourself commanded a company in the 1971 war, how do you see such a scenario play out?*

[CK] In such a scenario, the company under attack would require the entire divisional artillery support to check the attack.

What if no artillery support is available? Not just at the division level, but not even a single gun at the battalion level? Let us also assume that some mortar support is available. How would that scenario play out?

If the company only has mortar support, the enemy will pulverize their defences with overwhelming force.

Lastly, what options would the defending company commander have at that point, knowing fully well what is coming at him?

His option would be to either withdraw, or stay put and fight it out. If he chooses to fight, the survival rate would be nil.

7 a.m. (approximately)

In the rapidly deteriorating conditions at Point 303, he has few cards left to play. The handful of light mortars his men possess are of little use now as they are far too ineffective and far too few to shut off every approach available to the rapidly advancing attackers. And in any case, now there is no clear line for the mortars to target as the leading enemy troops have already reached his forwardmost squads and hand-to-hand fighting has broken out in the trenches.

As for countering the enemy tanks, the weapons his men possess that are capable of making an impression on a Sherman tank are not yielding any meaningful results. The couple of shoulder-fired bazooka rockets that his men possess can disable a Sherman if they strike it where the tank is most vulnerable—its tracks and its turret—but their limited range makes it hard for even his best marksmen to aim for the Sherman's weak points.

As for his lone remaining recoilless rifle (RR)—a larger version of the anti-tank bazooka mounted on a jeep for mobility—even though the RR's jeep crew valiantly drives through a curtain of gunfire in a spirited effort to target the Shermans, no enemy tank falls to them.[13]

A short while later . . .

The fog of smoke and dust engulfing Point 303 limits his visibility, but he knows what is coming his way now that one of his platoons has been overrun—the last communication from the platoon was that the enemy was upon them; now he is unable to hail them. At any moment now, enemy soldiers will swarm his command post in numbers that he and his two lightly armed men, radio operator Mohan Singh and Company Havildar Ajit Singh, will be unable to make much of an impression on. After that, all the dominoes will begin to fall: the enemy will make a run down the road leading to the brigade headquarters in Chhamb, then the division headquarters in Pallanwalla and finally, the strategically vital bridge at Akhnoor.

It is then that he plays his last remaining card. Over the wireless, he calls headquarters and gives Indian forces permission to bomb his very own post to smithereens. His intent is to take along all the enemy on the ridge with him as he goes down.

Then, over the din of gunfire spraying his post as enemy troops appear around it, he barks out his very last orders to his two companions to sprint back to headquarters to warn the commanders there of the peril they face now that his post has been overrun, as is about to happen that very instant.

Afterwards

It was Company Havildar Ajit Singh who would witness, and later recount, the last confirmed sighting of Captain Kamal Bakshi. After the captain had barked out orders for him to sprint back to headquarters, the havildar had rushed towards the rear exit of the trench, towards the gulley that led away from the ridge. And right before turning into the gulley, the havildar had turned around momentarily and had witnessed a sight he would later recount many times over: with a Sten machine gun at his hip—ablaze—Captain Bakshi had leapt out of the trench in the direction of the onrushing enemy.

ooo

A few weeks after the war, the Army would go on to award Captain Kamal Bakshi a posthumous 'Mention in Dispatches' in recognition of his courage and conduct in war. And some days later, word of Kamal's last stand would reach a news reporter who would go on to describe it in a popular weekly newsmagazine:

January 9, 1972
The Illustrated Weekly of India

From the Western Front
by
Jay Inder Kalra

. . . and there was Captain Kamal Bakshi . . . who was in command of a Company at Point 303. His Company was first attacked by their artillery and then attacked by a force of 30[14] tanks and more than a battalion of infantry. His platoons were overrun and yet he refused to retreat. When his entire Company was overrun, and the enemy tanks approached his headquarters, he called his commander on the radio: '. . . I am going into action . . . rat . . . tat . . . tat . . .' He charged into the enemy . . .

General Malhotra

(Lt. General J.L. Malhotra is a retired three-star Army general. He was Kamal's senior and his battalion's second-in-command during the war.)

[Author] *Sir, thank you so much for agreeing to meet me at a day's notice.*

[GM] You are late.

I apologize. I underestimated the time it takes to drive from Delhi.

So, what can I do for you, young man?

You were the last person to speak with Kamal over the wireless. I was hoping you could tell me more about that moment. I do realize it has been fifty years since that day and memories tend to fade . . .

Not my memory. I remember everything. Every little detail. Each December, I recount to my wife what happened in that war hour by hour, blow by blow.

    Kamal's last words to me were, 'The enemy is here. I am going on the attack.' His radio went dead after that. Just before that transmission, he had declared 'red-over-red-over-red'. That is code for asking your artillery to target your own position. A soldier can either say it over the radio like Kamal did, or fire off three red flares into the sky.

What happened after that?

The enemy captured Point 303 (his post). That was a very dangerous moment for our side because the road to Chhamb now lay open to the enemy. So right away, I organized a counter-attack. A troop of tanks and a company of Gorkhas were made available to me and I ordered the head of our MMG detachment, Subedar Narain Singh, to lead the counter-attack as he knew the terrain well. And we succeeded. Point 303 was back in our control by late morning.

Was there any sighting of Kamal?

None. Subedar Narain Singh personally led the search for Kamal but did not find him at his command post or within 100 yards of it.

○ ○ ○

Letters of condolences have been steadily arriving at his parents' house but his parents are in no mood to write back, for their grief is too profound, their sorrow too huge. One letter writer stands out in his persistence, and continues to write to them again and again and again:

Dear Colonel:

I had written to you from Shillong when I was in hospital there, but you probably did not receive that letter of mine. So I write again, and again, until I hear from you.

Kamal was, and is, the best friend I ever had. I felt very secure in his company and confided in him. I like to think that he trusted me as well. I do have all his letters with me and they shall remain my most treasured possessions until the day I meet him again.

I have known him now for almost ten years right from our NDA years. As our tastes were somewhat alike, we took a liking to each other and corresponded regularly right until the outbreak of the war. I was myself wounded in action—a bullet passed through my ankle when I successfully led a rifle company in assault against enemy strongholds. I have been in and out of hospitals ever since as the bullet has left a legacy to reckon with.

I still cannot reconcile to the fact that Kamal is lost forever. In losing him, we have lost a raw, rustic, humble, and true son of the motherland.

Knowing Kamal for almost ten years now, I know he would have fought to the last drop in him, unless of course he was injured and overpowered. Knowing his tenacity and determination, and his capacity to live off the land wherever he may be,

I still hope for a day he will come back and join us all. If he turns up at your door and says 'Hello Mum and Dad', please send me an express telegram. I shall fly down to meet him. It will be one of the greatest moments of my life. I won't even mind sacrificing my life in the next war if he is returned to you as he is definitely truer to the nation and worthier than me.

I have only one request. If you could be kind enough to send me a recent photo of Kamal's, it will find an honorable place in my album. He always resisted any attempts of others to photograph him and neither did he keep any photos of himself.

With love and regards,

Arjun

7

Nowhere Men
1972–Present

December 1971—January 1972

Captain (later Colonel) Anil Athale has come up with a number of ways to cope with the loneliness of being held in solitary confinement in a prison in Rawalpindi, Pakistan—he exercises regularly, thinks of his family and all the girls he knows back home, and tries to plot his escape from the prison. To that end, he quickly slips on his boots each time the anti-aircraft gun mounted atop the prison starts to fire at Indian Air Force jets flying overhead, his reasoning being that if the Indian jets return fire, they might create a breach in the prison wall through which he could escape.[1]

Another thought that occupies his mind is that he is not the only POW being detained there. He knows this because each morning he counts the number of prison doors that are unlocked by the guard handing over the day's meal to prisoners. By his reckoning, there are at least seven or eight POWs there, including himself.

But a month later, after he is released from solitary confinement and transferred to the main POW camp in Lyallpur, Pakistan, he will be in for a surprise. After comparing notes with other Indian prisoners in the camp, he will find that there is only one other prisoner there who had undergone solitary confinement in the same prison as he had.

'What happened to the other five or six prisoners?' he will wonder.[2]

[Author's Note: It appears that all the Indian Army and Air Force officers who were taken POW were sent up to prisons in Rawalpindi for interrogation. Several published accounts by Indian POWs mentions this fact.

If Kamal was among the POWs sent to Rawalpindi, his peripatetic life would have come full circle, for Rawalpindi is also the city where he was born.]

11 January 1972

It has been two days since the Indian representative to the International Committee of the Red Cross in Geneva has handed over a list of names of Pakistani POWs in Indian custody. Now, two days later, it is the Pakistanis who are handing over a list of Indian POWs they have in their custody.[3] When the list reaches India, telegrams will be sent off to families of soldiers whose names are on it.

His parents, however, will not be getting a telegram as his name is not on the list.

[Author's Note: As subsequent events presented in this book make clear, the list of Indian POWs handed over to the Red Cross on 11 January 1972 was incomplete.]

1 December 1972

From Agence France-Presse, a news bulletin:

Delhi: The Indian Government announced today that it would release on Friday all 540 Pakistani prisoners of war captured on the western front during last December's war. The prisoners will be handed over to Pakistani authorities at the border post of Wagah.

Meanwhile, an Indian source said that India had not received any information from the International Committee of the Red Cross, on 300 Indians who had been listed as missing on the western front. The Red Cross was asked six months ago to contact the Pakistani authorities about their whereabouts.

○○○

A crowd has gathered at the border checkpoint where the exchange of POWs is about to occur. At the appointed hour, the gates are pushed open, and two lines of men start streaming through them in opposite directions.

Among those standing off to the side is his father, wearing his trademark dark glasses and staring intently at each Indian soldier walking past. Although Kamal's name was not on the list that Pakistan had handed over to Red Cross officials, his father has not given up searching for him. Maybe there was a clerical error when the list was typed, his father had reasoned.

As the stream of men draws to an end, his father's eyes well up with tears. And when the last man crosses over and the checkpoint gates are slammed shut, tears roll down his cheeks from behind his dark glasses.

Perhaps he died on the battlefield during his charge through enemy gunfire, his father tells himself. Or perhaps he succumbed to his injuries in prison in the intervening period, his father thinks, as he discreetly wipes his face and walks away.

[Author's Note: This POW exchange was only for Indian and Pakistani soldiers captured on the western front.

The Pakistani soldiers captured by India in East Pakistan (now called Bangladesh) would be released sixteen months later, on 30 April 1974. At the heart of the long-drawn-out negotiations between India, Pakistan and Bangladesh was the fate of 195 Pakistani POWs that Bangladesh wanted to put on trial for war crimes against its people. Within days of the wars ending, Bangladeshis had started demanding that India hand over the Pakistani POWs to them, while Pakistan pressed India not to do so. Bangladesh and Pakistan resolved their differences in early 1974 when Bangladesh dropped its demand for war crimes trials in exchange for Pakistan recognizing the Bangladeshi Government.]

1979

In the recently held general elections in India, the ruling party has been voted out, and the new party in power has no qualms about disclosing the so-called national secrets that have hitherto been kept out of the public eye. This is about to happen in Parliament, where the Minister of State for External Affairs Shri Samarendra Kundu is ready to take the floor.

Minister Kundu had been questioned some months earlier about anecdotal reports of Indian POWs being illegally detained in Pakistan. Now, after reviewing government files, he announces that the Indian Government has reason to believe that some Indian military personnel were held back by Pakistan after the war even after India released over 93,000 Pakistani POWs, and among them is an Army captain named Kamal Bakshi.[4]

○○○

Newspapers take an unconventional route to reach McCluskieganj, the town where his parents now live. Since it is too small to merit a stop by the express train that passes by each morning, the most efficient way of delivering the daily newspaper to the handful of readers there is to toss a bundle of them from the fast-moving train on to the station platform. The bundle gets picked up by the nearby tea stall owner and is then distributed to subscribers when they drop by. And so it is that Om Prakash and Shanta learn that their son's name had been mentioned in the Indian Parliament; that the son they had lost to war seven years earlier might still be alive.

○○○

Now that the government has publicly acknowledged the illegal incarceration of Indian POWs by Pakistan, R.S. Suri has decided to break his silence: his son, Major Ashok Suri, is also listed as being detained in Pakistan, but unlike other relatives of the missing men, Suri has indisputable proof of his son's captivity in the form of two handwritten notes from his son.

The first note, dated 7 December 1974, was a slip of paper that simply said, 'I am okay here', and an accompanying letter from a gentleman named M. Abdul Hamid:

7-12-1974

Sahib,

Valaikumsalam. I cannot meet you in person. Your son is alive and he is in Pakistan. I could only bring this slip, which I am sending you. Now going back to Pak.

M Abdul Hamid

The second letter from Major Suri, written in June of 1975, was more detailed. Not only had it mentioned its city of origin, Karachi, but also that there were nineteen other Indian officers being held prisoner there, along with Major Suri.

Karachi
14-6-75
15-6-75
16-6-75

Dear Daddy.

Ashok touches thy feet to get a benediction.
I am quite OK here. Please try to contact Indian
Army or Govt of India about us. We are 20
officers here. Don't worry about me. Pay my
regards to everybody at home, especially mummy,
grandfather. Indian Govt can contact Pakistan
Govt for our freedom. Your loving son

A Kumar Suri

R.S. Suri had promptly shared the letters with top
Indian government officials, who, in turn, told Suri
that they wanted to run forensic checks on the letter to
verify the handwriting. 'Go right ahead,' R.S. Suri had
told them.

Then, after agreeing that the handwriting and
style of writing matched Major Suri's, the government
officials had told R.S. Suri to keep mum about
the sensitive matter while they carried out further
investigations.

But four years had passed since then, and the
Indian government had come up empty-handed.

So had R.S. Suri, after making various attempts to approach the Red Cross, Amnesty International and also a well-connected Pakistani businessman living in Canada whom Suri knew personally. So now, with the matter out in the open, he has decided to reach out to families of other missing soldiers to share everything he knows, starting with the letter from his son.

R.S. Suri would also go on to disclose that although the handwritten note from his son was the most credible proof of him surviving the war, it was not the only evidence he had on hand. Soon after learning of the odd circumstances under which his son had gone missing in battle, he had begun tapping into his extensive network of high-placed government officials, seeking answers, and discovered different accounts of the event. One was that the convoy of trucks his son was leading had disappeared; another said that he had died in a field hospital, although there was no record of his death. And just three months after the war's ending, he had learnt something that had stunned him. An Indian diplomat—whose name Suri does not divulge—had received a cable from his western contact saying: 'About Suri, I have informed you before and have nothing more to say. His name was among the list of wounded soldiers, and he was in good shape. No further information is possible. His number is OK. Will inform you if any information is available again!'[5]

[Author's Note: It is revealing to note that the first letter from Major Ashok Suri arrived eight months after India

had released the last Pakistani POW. The messenger of the letter, a Pakistani citizen named M. Abdul Hamid, was obviously troubled by the fact that his country was still holding on to Indian POWs after India had repatriated all Pakistani POWs. For his rectitude and his courage, the author has dedicated this book to the same M. Abdul Hamid.]

1988–98

India and Pakistan have just conducted another prisoner swap at the same border checkpoint where POWs were exchanged sixteen years earlier. This time, however, the repatriates are civilians incarcerated for crimes ranging from unintentionally straying across the border while herding cattle to intentionally crossing over for smuggling or espionage. Among the repatriated is Mukhtiar Singh, a man who has spent over a decade in Pakistani prisons to serve time for his alleged crime.

When debriefed by Indian authorities at the border on 5 July 1988 about his time in prison, Mukhtiar will claim to have met an Indian Army officer named Captain Kamal Bakshi.

It will be over a year after Mukhtiar's repatriation that Kamal's parents will learn of his sighting in a prison in Pakistan.

[Author's Note: Kamal's parents learnt of Mukhtiar Singh's claim from the well-connected R.S. Suri in late 1989, a year after Mukhtiar's repatriation. Suri, in turn, learnt of

Mukhtiar Singh's debriefing either from his sources in the Ministry of External Affairs, or from L.D. Kaura (father of Captain Ravinder Kaura).

In addition to mentioning Captain Kamal Bakshi, Mukhtiar Singh also claimed to have met Captain Ravinder Kaura (the same artillery observation officer who was embedded with the platoon in Moel, mentioned earlier in this book) multiple times in several prisons across Pakistan. Before Mukhtiar's repatriation to India, Captain Kaura had given Mukhtiar his family's address in Delhi. After getting repatriated, Mukhtiar wrote a letter to Captain Kaura's father in March 1989 and the two subsequently met.]

○○○

Subedar Assa Singh's family has always believed that he died in battle. Nor was his name on the list of POWs released in Parliament in 1979. But now, seventeen years after the war, his family has been thrown into a tizzy, for a man has just showed up at their house claiming otherwise. He says his name is Mohinder Lal, and that he had been repatriated from Pakistan a month earlier after serving time there on charges of spying. Before being arrested by the Pakistanis, his cover was that of a mason, he says, and it was while working at a military hospital in Multan that he had met Assa Singh.

Assa Singh's son will ask the unexpected guest if he is willing to get his statement recorded at the local army barracks, and the guest will agree. But nothing will come of it—no formal inquiry and no investigation of the lead provided by Mohinder Lal. Instead, Mohinder Lal will be harassed by the local authorities and ridiculed for making up tales, and in due course, he will break contact with Assa Singh's family, leaving them to wonder if he was indeed telling the truth.

But they will stop wondering several years later when another stranger will show up at their house. He will say his name is Bhogal Ram, that he too had served time in a Pakistani jail and that he had seen Assa Singh as recently as 1998. He will admit that he had not spoken with Assa Singh personally, but instead had learnt of his identity from a prison guard. As per Bhogal Ram, when he had told the prison guard he was from a village near Jammu, the prison guard had let on that the old man in the adjoining cell was also from a village near Jammu and that his name was Assa Singh.

[Author's Note: Subedar Assa Singh was from the same battalion as Captain Bakshi and the two knew each another. Assa Singh's company was positioned on the northern end of the Phagla ridge, while Captain Bakshi's was 3000 yards away on the southern end.]

○○○

It is not unusual for a newly elected liberal-minded first-term politician to speak with candour, for that is when their idealism and desire to right previous wrongs are strongest. With time, however, reality sets in and like most seasoned politicians, they learn to be more guarded in their responses.

An example of this had occurred during Pakistani Prime Minister Benazir Bhutto's first term in office. Just twenty-eight days after being elected in December 1988, she had been questioned by her Indian counterpart in a joint news conference about the missing POWs. She had answered in earnest that she had heard of Indian POWs being held in a Pakistani jail and would seriously look into their release.[6]

Her frankness, however, had not lasted long. The Pakistani military junta had vilified her for cosying up to the enemy (India), among other things, and a year and a half after being elected, she had been sacked from the job. In her second term as prime minister starting in 1993, Bhutto would go on to take a more guarded tack in her public comments about India.

2011

With the brief exception of Benazir Bhutto, early in her first term as prime minister, the Pakistani leadership has been remarkably consistent in dismissing pleas for the release of Indian POWs. To this end, they have always used a clever rhetorical argument along the lines of, 'If you don't like the message, discredit the messenger', their argument being that reports of Indian POWs in Pakistani jails are false because the men making these claims are ex-felons, spies, smugglers and thieves who cannot be trusted.

But something incredible is about to unfold on a remote island off the Arabian Peninsula that will make the Pakistani argument irrelevant, and will cause families of missing Indian soldiers to stare at the world atlas in bewilderment.

A government-owned facility on Masirah Island in Oman requires the services of a carpenter, and the authorities have contracted the job out to a civilian firm. The firm, in turn, has assigned the task to Sukhdev Singh, a migrant worker from India. As instructed, each morning, Sukhdev makes his way to the parking lot of the Shell petrol station near the entrance to the Masirah Air Force base, where he is met by a local who escorts him to a building with armed guards, where cabinets need to be installed in the kitchen.

Sukhdev works alone and keeps to himself during the course of the day, but occasionally an old man—bearded and skull-capped—drops by the kitchen to prepare tea. At the end of his shift, Sukhdev's escort returns and accompanies him back to the Shell petrol station, from where he finds his way to his lodgings for the night.

His daily visits to the kitchen remain uneventful at first but then take an unexpected turn when the old man—after making sure no one is within earshot—turns to him and speaks in a hushed tone in Punjabi:

'I too am a Sikh, like you,' the old man says, recognizing the Sikh-style turban that Sukhdev wears.

Sukhdev is puzzled at being spoken to in Punjabi by a foreigner, but what the old man tells him next astonishes him. The old man says that his name is Jaspal Singh and that he was an Indian soldier who had been taken prisoner in 1971 after his company had been overrun by the enemy in the battle for Hussainiwala. After being held captive in a Pakistani prison for four years, he, along with a number of other Indians, had been shipped to Masirah Island by boat. Out of the group, only he and one other prisoner were being held at that facility. Where the other prisoners had been taken, he does not know.

It is a fantastical tale and Sukhdev is rightfully sceptical, until their next exchange.

'Which village in Punjab are you from?' the old man asks Sukhdev.

'Village Dugri, near Ropar,' says Sukhdev.

'I know that village. My wife's village is not very far from yours,' says the old man, before going on to name some people who live there.

ooo

A group comprising journalists, a retired Army officer and the kin of two of the missing POWs are seated inside Sukhdev's home and are listening to him recount his fortuitous encounter with the POW.[7] After meeting the old man, Sukhdev had remained in Oman for another year, as was stipulated by his contract. Then, one day, after returning to India on 12 July 2012, he had ridden his bicycle over to the neighbouring village, which the old man had mentioned. After inquiring about the family of a soldier from the 1971 war, he had been directed to the house where the old man's wife now lived.

After hearing him out, the old man's wife had disappeared into her house and returned with a framed photograph of her long-dead husband. 'Was he the man you spoke to?' she had asked Sukhdev. 'Yes, it was him,' Sukhdev had conceded.

○○○

A group of protesters have gathered outside the gates of the Embassy of Oman in New Delhi and are demanding an answer. 'Why has the country, which India considers a close ally, been holding Indian soldiers in prison for over forty years?' they ask.

A few kilometres away, officials of the Ministry of External Affairs are also scratching their heads, mulling over the same question.

2017

Five years have passed since an Indian POW was spotted in a prison in Oman and there has been no word from the authorities about his case since then. But now, after being forced to respond to an RTI (right to information) request filed by a newspaper publisher, the authorities make this brief statement:[8]

As per the information received from the local authorities, there is no detention centre in Masirah Wilayat and no Indian national was detained in Masirah island jail of Oman.

As to why an investigation cannot be conducted of the premises where the soldier was last seen, irrespective of whether it is a detention centre or an administrative building, and irrespective of what name he was registered under, be it Jaspal or Jalal or Jack, the authorities do not say.

Kiki and Niki

[Author] *Mrs Bakshi and Mrs Kumar, I confess that when I first heard of your brother's case, I did not believe the funny business about his captivity. I have changed my mind now.*

[K and N] What made you change your mind?

It all made sense to me when I understood the Pakistani motive for making some Indian POWs disappear.

Why did they do it?

To use them as bargaining chips in post-war negotiations with India. Plain and simple. All the facts are clearly reported in foreign newspapers. One just has to connect the dots to reveal the bigger picture.

You see, as soon as the war ended, the Bangladeshis started hounding the Indians to hand over hundreds of Pakistani officers accused of committing war crimes against the Bengalis. Indian authorities, for their part, dithered: they neither confirmed nor denied their intentions to hand over the war criminals, infuriating the Bangladeshis and terrifying the Pakistanis. All this is noted in a New York Times article from 26 December 1971.

Around the same time, Swiss officials from the Red Cross started pressurizing Pakistani and Indian authorities to quickly hand over lists of POWs in their custody. All this is described in detail in the Red Cross Bulletin dated January 1972.

So what does the Pakistani leadership do, while under pressure from the Red Cross, and fearing that India will hand over some of their men to the Bangladeshis?

They hold back some of our men?

Exactly! They withhold names of some Indian POWs from the list that they submit to the Red Cross. Those POWs are to be their trump card, their leverage in case the Indians hand over their men to Bangladeshis for war crime trials.

But why not release our men once it was agreed that there would not be any war crimes trials? Why keep our men locked up forever?

Because then they would have had to admit to handing over an incomplete list of Indian POWs to the Red Cross. It takes integrity and courage to admit one's own mistake. Something that was obviously lacking among the leaders.

There was one other thing I wanted to ask you both—how did your parents come to learn of your brother's disappearance?

Our parents were living in an encampment in Himachal Pradesh where my father was commanding a battalion of the Indo-Tibetan Border Police. It was my father who read the telegram from the Defence Ministry first. As per my mother, he immediately left his office, walked over to the tent where she was and broke down when he saw her.

It must have been agonizing for them . . .

It was. The light went out of their lives. Dad took retirement soon after the event, and they settled in a small town in the hinterland to rebuild their lives. The day-to-day business of settling in a new home and renovating it to make it comfortable for themselves, returned a sense of normalcy to their lives, but their hearts were broken—my brother was constantly on their minds! Being spiritual, they stayed on the side of hope, even as they looked for ways to cope with their grief. Dad threw himself into books, especially his new interest, homeopathy. He had done a correspondence course in the past few years, and got busy treating people in the area, free of charge. Every morning saw a fair number of people gathered outside, visiting him to get treated. My mum developed a vegetable garden where she grew all sorts of veggies and legumes. But in their free moments, they were reminded of the deep new wound fate had inflicted upon them, not only taking away from their joy of retirement, but leaving them in tears and extreme sadness.

Oftentimes, when sitting on their front veranda having their evening cup of tea, their eyes would turn towards the long driveway to the house, and one or the other would say: 'Wouldn't it be something if Kuku were to suddenly walk in through the gate right now?' Kuku was his nickname—that's what we all called him.

Once, in an upbeat state of mind, my mother even said: 'I wish I could send him a parcel wherever he is. I would send over a set of bagpipes for him to play his sweet music to people around him to bring them joy.'

And what about you, Mrs Bakshi?

It has been a lifelong struggle to contain the deep pain of losing my only brother, one who had such a large presence in my life. It isn't just about missing his physical presence—there is also the constant agony of wondering what happened on that fateful morning in 1971, and circular thoughts and questions continue to swirl in the mind, whether he is all right wherever he is, and whether he'll still return one day, and we'll meet . . . there are so many stories from war-torn areas where people have met after fifty, sixty, even seventy years!

I know our family is not unique in living through a tragedy such as this, but when someone goes missing, it is different than them dying. In death, one has to work towards finding a closure. There is a psychological term for what we went through, and are still going through—it is called 'ambiguous loss'. Here, there is no closure, and the loss continues to shape its sufferers, completely and continually moulding their lives.

And you, Mrs Kumar?

I miss him very much. He was the best brother a sister could ever wish for. I am still hopeful of meeting him again. There is a human-rights lawyer[9] here in London who is helping me pursue his case with officials at the UN. Even my brother's schoolmates are seeking answers about his whereabouts. I was fortunate to meet them all when they invited me to their fifty-year school reunion a few years back. They live all over the world now, and yet they are continuing to pursue my brother's case.

Perhaps he will return home someday. And why not? Stranger things have happened. And when he does, he will have one hell of a story to tell. One to rival that of Odysseus!

Epilogue

The search for Kamal has hitherto been a long and uphill journey. It is still continuing, even though each of the leads followed so far has only led to one dead end after another!

Soon after receiving a telegram from the Army that Kamal had been reported killed, his father travelled to his battalion to find out first-hand what had happened to his son. What he learnt there was not what the telegram had said. No one in Kamal's unit had seen him get killed, nor found his body later, even though the telegram had said 'Killed in action'. So, Kamal's father began his quest to have his son's status changed from 'Killed in Action' to 'Missing in Action'; his reasoning being that if he could get the Army to acknowledge his son as being missing, he could then press the Ministry of Defence to investigate his son's subsequent disappearance.

However, his appeals went nowhere. One brigadier wrote back, 'As an Army officer yourself, you ought to know the realities of battle—sometimes bodies cannot be recovered.' The brigadier did have a point. Gruesome acts occur in battle all the time—sometimes men get run over by a tank, leaving no trace of them. Kamal's father agreed with this possibility, but the fact remained that no one had seen his son get killed, and therefore his status must say 'missing'.

Kamal's father's disagreement with the Army became a moot point in 1979, when the Indian government by its own admission announced that Kamal, along with several other Indian soldiers, was being detained in Pakistan. Thereafter, he joined forces with R.S. Suri and the families of other missing POWs, to appeal to government officials to act. But again, their efforts did not bear fruit. The answer they got from the officials was always the same—'Pakistan denies the existence of the POWs, so there is nothing we can do.'

Since the passing of Kamal's parents, his sisters continued to appeal to government officials and to NGOs, such as Amnesty International. Their efforts got a big boost in the summer of 2012, when Kamal's classmates from Sherwood College met for their fifty-year reunion in India. As Kamal was unreachable, the batch of 1962 invited Kamal's sister, Niki, to participate in the celebration. It was from her that many of them learnt about Kamal being on the list of missing soldiers, and of being sighted in a Pakistani prison as recently as the late 1980s.

The shocking news of this sighting of Kamal, and just two months after the reunion, the news of an Indian soldier from the 1971 war being discovered in a prison in Oman, galvanized Kamal's outraged classmates. They launched a worldwide effort of their own, to bring their friend back home. Looking for information, Australia-based Brian McMahon tried contacting high-ranking officials everywhere, including some Pakistani military officers. He even made an appeal to the President of India, to initiate a dialogue with the Pakistani government to resolve this matter once and for all. Thakur Patel, a doctor in the US Navy, published an article about Kamal's situation in a periodical in the US. Ian Atkinson presented Kamal's case to a retired high court judge in Australia. All in the hope that international pressure may be put on the government of Pakistan to release the Indian POWs.

The collective effort of Kamal's classmates also played a role in propelling me to write this book. To see a fine group of gentlemen taking up a cause they believed in, against all odds, was very inspirational to me. As for the search for Kamal, just as it happened to others before me, each supposedly promising lead I examined and explored led to a dead end.

Recently, my hopes rose when I learnt that the International Committee of the Red Cross (ICRC) was allowing public viewing of their archives of all wars fought the world over before 1975. However, when I contacted them to set up an appointment to view the records pertaining to POWs of the 1971 Indo–Pak war, I was told that there was one exception to the opening of the archives—that being the very records I was interested in. Why this is so remains unclear. The ICRC authorities assured me that the sealed records do not contain any information on Captain Kamal Bakshi, but even so, one cannot help but wonder just what is in those records that the authorities want to keep shielded from the public, even though more than fifty years have passed since that war ended—why only those few records, compared to the thousands that were unsealed. Surely time will tell!

> *'Three things cannot be long hidden: the sun,*
> *the moon, and the truth'*
>   —The Buddha

A Timeline of POW Negotiations
and Sightings

Date	News report/Event	Author's comments
16 December 1971	**Ceasefire declared**	
26 December 1971	**India Weighs Bengali Pleas to Try Pak Officials** *New York Times* 'India is uncertain whether to hand over the former leaders of the Pakistani Government here 'to Bangladesh officials for trial as war criminals, India's special envoy here indicated today . . . More and more, irate Bengalis are demanding that the Indian Army let them try the former Pakistani leaders of East Pakistan.'	*India found itself between a rock and a hard place immediately after the war ended: on one hand, Bangladesh was demanding that it hand over Pakistani soldiers accused of war crimes. On the other hand, it did not want to anger Pakistan as there was a long list of items that needed to be negotiated with the Pakistanis, including the fate of Indian POWs in Pakistani custody.*

Date	News report/Event	Author's comments
9 January 1972	**India and Pakistan Submit List of POWs** International Review of the Red Cross, February 1972 'As regards information about prisoners of war, an ICRC delegate, on his return to Geneva, handed the Agency on 9 January 1972 the preliminary lists of Pakistani prisoners of war held by the Indians. The lists were immediately recorded and promptly forwarded to the Government of Pakistan through its Geneva representative. Two days later, the Agency received from the ICRC delegate at Islamabad a list of Indian prisoners of war held by the Pakistanis. This list, too, was recorded and handed to the Indian Permanent Delegation in Geneva for transmission to the Government of India.'	*We now know that Pakistani authorities submitted an incomplete list of Indian POWs to the Red Cross. As for why they did it, the obvious answer, as the news articles presented in this timeline make clear, was to use the Indian POWs as bargaining chips in case India handed over some Pakistani POWs to the Bangladeshis for war crimes trials.*

continued

Date	News report/Event	Author's comments
18 March 1972	**India Opens Way for Dacca Trials** *New York Times* 'The Indian Government said tonight that all Pakistani military prisoners against whom Bangladesh presents "prima facie cases" of atrocities and similar crimes would be turned over to the Bangladesh Government for war-crimes trials. This statement—the furthest the Indians have gone to satisfy Dacca on one of the thorniest issues on the subcontinent—was made by an Indian spokesman as Prime Minister Indira Gandhi began her first visit to the new Bengali nation that she helped create.'	*Pakistani officials could have used this news as further justification for withholding names of Indian POWs from the list they handed to the Red Cross two months earlier.*

Date	News report/Event	Author's comments
30 March 1972	**Bangladesh Will Try 1,100 Pakistanis** *New York Times* 'Accusing India and Bangladesh of using the prisoners as blackmail to win concessions from Pakistan at eventual peace talks, Mr. Bhutto said recently that if Bangladesh put Pakistani soldiers on trial for war crimes, "then I am afraid we would be reaching the point of no return".'	*Now that we know for certain that Pakistani officials withheld names of some Indian POWs, this statement from Prime Minister Zulfikar Bhutto raises a troubling question: What exactly did he mean by 'point of no return'? Was be referring to the return of Indian POWs whose names were withheld from the Red Cross?*

continued

Date	News report/Event	Author's comments
14 June 1972	**India to Deliver 150 POWs to Bangladesh to Face Trial** *New York Times* 'India has agreed to give 150 Pakistani prisoners of war to Bangladesh for interrogation and trial on charges of genocide, a Foreign Ministry official said here today.'	*India made this statement a couple of weeks before Pakistani President Bhutto was to arrive in Simla to begin negotiation talks. It probably did so to increase pressure on Bhutto to come to a settlement.* *However, once again, Pakistani officials probably saw this as justification for holding back names of some Indian POWs.*
29 July 1972	**India Ratifies Pakistan Pact** *New York Times* 'The agreement, signed in Simla between Prime Minister Indira Gandhi of India and President Zulfikar Ali Bhutto of Pakistan on July 2, will take effect when the Indian instrument of ratification reaches Rawalpindi in two days. Pakistan has already ratified it.'	*Also called the Simla Agreement, this pact was a peace treaty between India and Pakistan, and set the framework around which further negotiations were to take place to resolve all open issues, including POW repatriation. In hindsight, this was another missed opportunity for India to ensure all its POWs were accounted for before signing this agreement.*

Date	News report/Event	Author's comments
29 November 1972	**POWs to Be Freed Friday** *New York Times* 'The Indian Government announced today that it would release on Friday all 540 Pakistani prisoners of war captured on the western front during last December's war. Pakistan has already announced that she was releasing the 617 Indians taken prisoner in the fighting . . . India still holds more than 90,000 Pakistani troops taken prisoner during the fighting (on the Bangladeshi front) . . . An Indian source said, meanwhile, that India had received no information from the International Committee of Red Cross on 300 Indians who had been listed as missing on the western front in the December fighting. The Red Cross was asked six months ago to contact the Pakistani authorities about their whereabouts.'	*This exchange was only for prisoners of the western front. Captain Kamal Bakshi should have been a part of this exchange.*

continued

Date	News report/Event	Author's comments
31 January 1973	**90,000 Prisoners** *New York Times* 'India claims it cannot release the prisoners (from the Bangladeshi front) without the concurrence of Bangladesh . . . Bangladesh says it won't agree to prisoner release until Islamabad recognizes the Dacca Government.'	*This is referring to the Pakistani prisoners of war captured in East Pakistan (now called Bangladesh).*

Date	News report/Event	Author's comments
7 April 1974	**India Talks Hinge on POW Issue** *New York Times* 'The fate of 195 Pakistani prisoners emerged as the pivotal issue today at the meeting of foreign ministers of India, Pakistan and Bangladesh . . . These prisoners have been listed by Bangladesh for possible war crimes trials . . . Prime Minister Zulfikar Ali Bhutto of Pakistan has demanded the return of all the Pakistani prisoners of war, including the 195. The Pakistani delegation here has indicated that the issue must be resolved before the three nations settle down to further discussions.'	*This news, once again, shows that the fate of Pakistani POWs accused of war crimes was the central issue of post-war negotiations. And once again, Pakistani officials would have used this as justification for their decision to withhold names of some Indian POWs from the list they handed over to the Red Cross after the war.*

continued

Date	News report/Event	Author's comments
10 April 1974	**India, Bangladesh and Pakistan End Prisoner Dispute** *New York Times* 'India, Pakistan and Bangladesh reached a major breakthrough tonight and signed an agreement to repatriate 195 Pakistani prisoners of war . . . It was learned however, that the war crimes trial planned for the Pakistani prisoners by Bangladesh, the former eastern wing of Pakistan, would be dropped.'	*This is the moment the fate of the missing Indian POWs was sealed. Indian officials did not have any leverage for negotiating their release after this point.*
1 May 1974	**India Completes Return of Pakistani Prisoners** *New York Times* 'India released the last groups of Pakistani prisoners of war today, completing the return of 93,000 Pakistanis who were held in India for over two years.'	*This was Pakistan's opportunity to come clean. With all their POWs freed, they could have easily released the Indians they had held back. Unfortunately, they chose not to, as the following events make clear.*

Date	News report/Event	Author's comments
7 December 1974	**First letter from Major Ashok Suri to his father, R.S. Suri** Text on slip: 'I am okay here' Text on note: 'Sahib, valaikumsalam. I cannot meet you in person. Your son is alive and he is in Pakistan. I could only bring this slip, which I am sending you. Now going back to Pak. M Abdul Hamid.'	*At least one honourable Pakistani citizen named M. Abdul Hamid (likely an alias) believed that it was wrong for Pakistan to keep holding Indian POWs after India had returned all remaining Pakistani POWs earlier that year.*

continued

Date	News report/Event	Author's comments
13 June 1975	**Second letter from Major Ashok Suri to his father, R.S. Suri** 'Dear Daddy. Ashok touches thy feet to get a benediction. I am quite OK here. Please try to contact Indian Army or Govt of India about us. We are 20 officers here. Don't worry about me. Pay my regards to everybody at home, especially mummy, grandfather. Indian Govt can contact Pakistan Govt for our freedom. Your loving son. A. Kumar Suri'	*Clear proof that at least twenty Indian military officers were being detained in Pakistan after India had released all Pakistani POWs.* *It is also interesting to note that the letter originated in Karachi, and not some city in the hinterland of Pakistan, where it would have been easier to keep the POWs hidden.* *Sometime between 1972 and 1974, Inspector General of the Border Security Force Ashwini Kumar had learnt from his contacts in Pakistan that some Indian POWs were being detained secretly, outside the purview of Red Cross officials, in prisons on the Pakistan–Afghanistan border.* *Why would Pakistani officials shift them from a remote location on the Afghan border to Karachi which lies on the Arabian Sea coast? Were they trying to ship the men out of the country by sea?*

Date	News report/Event	Author's comments
1976–77	**At least three Indian POWs transferred by sea from Pakistan to Oman** (See 23 September 2012 news report below)	*As noted in the TV news link of 23 September 2012 provided in this table, Sepoy Jaspal Singh told the carpenter that he and four other soldiers were imprisoned in Pakistan for five or six years before being transferred to Oman by sea. That means Jaspal and his companions were shipped to Oman in 1976 or 1977.*
12 April 1979	The Government of India releases a list of names of Indian military personnel still believed to be in Pakistani custody. Included in the list is Captain Kamal Bakshi.	*No comment*

continued

Date	News report/Event	Author's comments
1980s onwards	Several civilian prisoners repatriated to India mention meeting or seeing or hearing about Indian Army POWs in prisons across Pakistan.	*No comment*
5 July 1988	Mukhtiar Singh, a civilian prisoner repatriated to India on 5 July 1988, claims to have seen Captain Kamal Bakshi in prison in Pakistan.	*No comment*
23 September 2012	Television news report about the existence of an Indian POW in a prison in Oman https://www.youtube.com/watch?v=gnlc4y26U1g	*No comment*

Suggested Further Reading

Battle of Chhamb from Indian viewpoint

- *Battleground Chhamb: The Indo-Pakistan War of 1971*, A.J.S. Sandhu, 2018
- *Portrait of Courage, Century of the 5th Battalion, The Sikh Regiment*, Prem K. Khanna and Pushpindar Singh Chopra, 2001
- *Indian Gunners at War, the Western Front—1971*, Jagjit Singh, 1994

Battle of Chhamb from Pakistani viewpoint

- *The Battle of Chhamb (1971)*, Ahmad Saeed, 1973
- *Forged in the Furnace of Battle*, Syed Ali Hamid, 2014

Missing Indian POWs

- *Missing in Action: The Prisoners Who Never Came Back*, Chander Suta Dogra, HarperCollins, 2019

Captain Kamal Bakshi in September 1971, three months before the war, at his younger sister's wedding.

Notes

Chhamb

1 Ahmad Saeed, *The Battle of Chhamb (1971)*, Army Education Press, 1973.

Early Years: 1945–1953

1 Kamal Ram, Wikipedia. Accessed 18 March 2023, https://en.wikipedia.org/wiki/Kamal_Ram.
2 A 6000-men-strong Indian Custodian Force was deployed to Korea between 1953 and 1954 to oversee the repatriation of prisoners of war.

Boyhood: 1954–1962

1 The Asian Flu Pandemic of 1957. Up to 4 million
   people are believed to have died from it worldwide.

Youth: 1963–1967

1 Injun was a distortion in the pronunciation, and
   thus in the spelling, of Indian, as in Native Indians.
   It is not pejorative.
2 William H. Bates, *Better Eyesight without Glasses*,
   Henry Holt and Company, New York, 1943.
3 Named after the Chindits special operations units of
   the British and Indian armies, which saw action in
   1943–1944, during the Burma Campaign of World
   War II.
4 Ralph Waldo Emerson (1803–1882) was a
   philosopher who led the Transcendentalism
   movement of the mid-nineteenth century. He was
   a champion of individualism and a critic of the
   pressures of society.

Soldiering: 1968–1970

1 *A Death in the Gunj* is a 2016 drama film written
   and directed by Konkona Sen Sharma. It won
   three awards at the 2018 Filmfare Awards—best
   cinematography, best costume design and best
   debut director. A trailer of the film can be seen here:
   https://www.youtube.com/watch?v=XliKkuxa_nA

2 General Hari Singh Nalwa (1791–1837) was the commander-in-chief of Maharaja Ranjit Singh's army.

3 Eminent Sherwoodians: Field Marshal S.H.F.J. Manekshaw, Old Sherwoodians. Accessed 18 March 2023, http://www.oldsherwoodians.com/ greats/index.htm?http://www.oldsherwoodians. com/greats/sam.htm.

The Approaching Storm: 1971

1 Sand models are 3D scale models of a tract of land, including trees, streams, etc. They are used for military training in tactics and artillery.

2 Pakistani accounts of the Battle of Chhamb refer to Point 303 as Point 994 (303 metres = 994 feet).

The Longest Hours: 3–6 December 1971

1 Indian intelligence grossly underestimated Pakistani strength in Chhamb. As would soon become clear to the Indians, the actual enemy strength was five brigades, not one.

2 Lieutenant General Baljit Singh, who was then an artillery officer, recalls that opening barrage in an essay titled 'Memories of the Chhamb Battle', *Indian Defence Review*, 11 September 2018, as follows: '. . . [Pakistan's] intelligence of our deployments (particularly west of Munnawar Tawi) and the ensuing intensity and precision of their

opening artillery concentrations was enviable. The softening up and in many cases pulverization of our BOPs (Border Observation Posts) and the Forward Defended Localities (FDLs) by Pak Artillery fire in the first two hours, made the task of their Infantry a mere cakewalk . . . Our fire targeted at Pak depth areas was more speculative than precise . . . It did not require a military deliberation to arrive at the obvious conclusion, that in the Chhamb Sector Pakistan had achieved surprise, both tactical and strategic.'

3 In his book *Battleground Chhamb: The Indo–Pakistan War of 1971*, Major General A.J.S. Sandhu reckons that Pakistan brought more artillery guns to the 24 km-long battlefront of Chhamb than they had in all of East Pakistan (now called Bangladesh).

4 The credit for the accurate artillery firing goes to Captain Ravinder Kaura, the artillery observation officer attached to the platoon in Moel. For his contributions in helping thwart the enemy's progress, the Indian Army would go on to award him a posthumous Vir Chakra.

5 In his book titled *The Battle of Chhamb*, Lieutenant Colonel Ahmed Saeed of the Pakistani Army acknowledges the critical role played by the Indian platoon in Moel thus: '. . . In all fairness, this enemy platoon fought extremely well and with great determination. By interposing itself between 3 Frontier Force and 42 Punjab, thus preventing

a junction between the two, the Platoon's contribution in holding the advance of the whole Brigade was great.'

6 In his book *Forged in the Furnace of Battle*, Major General Ali (Pakistan Army) mentions one Indian T-55 tank on the ridge getting hit.

7 Air Commodore Kaiser Tufail (PAF) writes in his blog: 'Three squadrons of F-86E/F at Sargodha, Munir and Peshawar made up the fighter element for air support of Chhamb Sector . . . The first phase of [Pakistani] 23 Division Operations that lasted from 4–7 December was vigorously supported by the PAF.'

8 Major-General A.J.S. Sandhu recounts the carnage at Kacheral in his book *Battleground Chhamb*.

9 Major Pannu's last words were recounted by Havildar Ajit Singh and reported on All India Radio by Melville de Mellow.

10 Lieutenant Colonel Ahmed Saeed of the Pakistan Army relates that fight in his book thus: 'The attack began at 1800 hours to capture Point 994 (Indians refer to it as Point 303). The leading companies of 10 Baluch moved forward. Enemy resistance was stiff and determined. Through a rain of bullets, the Battalion managed to close in. After a hand to hand fight the assaulting echelon gained a foothold on the high ground and thus

Point 994 changed hands for the first time in a long drawn-out duel which was to follow. But the [Indian] fire from Phagla ridge was deadly. Soon after, the enemy counter-attacked the position. Running low on ammunition which failed to reach up and under heavy pressure, 10 Baluch fell back. Enemy retook the position and for the second time Point 994 went to the enemy [Indian] hands.'

11 Mention must also be made of the help A Company got from the 18th Field Regiment artillery on that fateful evening of 5 December 1971. While the men of A Company were busy fighting off attackers who made it up the ridge, an artillery battery under the command of Captain Sukhwant Singh Gill was busy wreaking havoc on the enemy troops at the base of the ridge. For his action in Chhamb, Gill was later awarded the Vir Chakra.

12 In his book *Indian Gunners at War*, Major General Jagjit Singh explained the decision to pull back artillery as follows: 'In view of increasing enemy pressure, it was now clear that Pakistan had launched a major offensive in Chhamb. The following orders were issued to meet the situation: Guns west of the Tawi to withdraw east of the river.'

13 A Pakistani account of that battle described in the book *Forged in the Furnace of Battle* reports

one Pakistani tank getting hit by a high-explosive anti-tank (HEAT) round, injuring the tank commander. But the tank had remained operable as the round had made a glancing blow to the tank, bouncing off its side and spraying molten metal over it from the round's impact. As there were no Indian tanks supporting A Company that morning, it is quite possible that the HEAT round was fired from a recoilless rifle.

14 The actual number of tanks that attacked Point 303 on the morning of 6 December 1971 was a squadron worth—approximately fifteen tanks.

Nowhere Men: 1972–Present

1 Colonel Anil A. Athale (retd), 'My Days as a Prisoner of War in Pakistan', Rediff, 27 February 2019, https://www.rediff.com/news/special/my-days-as-a-prisoner-of-war-in-pakistan/20161216.htm.

2 Personal email exchange between the author and Colonel Athale.

3 International Review of the Red Cross, No. 131, February 1972, p. 89.

4 Minister Samarendra Kundu's response on 12 April 1979 to question 6803 asked by Amar Singh Pathwa in the Lok Sabha.

5 Chander Suta Dogra, *Missing in Action*, HarperCollins, 2019.

6 Benazir's admission of knowing about Indian POWs was not surprising because eight years prior to that, in 1980, her British friend Victoria Schofield had published a book about Bhutto's father's trial and execution. In her book, Schofield had quoted a letter written by the older Bhutto in which he said that fifty-odd Indian POWs were lodged in the cell next to his.

7 Headlines Today, 'Sepoy Jaspal Singh Traced after 41 Years', YouTube video, 23 September 2012, https://www.youtube.com/watch?v=gnlc4y26U1g.

8 Abhinandan Mishra, 'No Indian PoW in Oman Prison, Says Indian Embassy', the *Sunday Guardian*, 19 March 2017, https://www.sundayguardianlive.com/news/8790-no-indian-POW-oman-prison-says-indian-embassy.

9 Jas Uppal is a human rights lawyer based in the UK. She is also the founding trustee of Justice Upheld, a British-registered international human rights charity that provides legal help and representation to victims of human rights abuses.